"The Noblest Roman of Them All"—Champion Alford's John

HOW TO TRAIN YOUR BIRD DOG

BY

HORACE LYTLE

A. F. HOCHWALT COMPANY
DAYTON, OHIO

Grateful acknowledgment and deep appreciation are hereby extended to *Field & Stream* and to *The Saturday Evening Post* for permission to use in this book material previously prepared for and used in these magazines.

The Author

MANUFACTURED COMPLETE BY
KINGSPORT PRESS, Inc.
KINGSPORT, TENNESSEE
United States of America

DEDICATION

I dedicate this book to *The American Field,* a journal of the highest ideals—with a proud past and a splendid future.

H. L.

CONTENTS

ILLUSTRATIONS

FACING PAGE

FOREWORD

It is the writer's firm conviction that the training of a Bird Dog is not so much a matter of rule, as of *art*. Some men will fail utterly even when trying to accomplish a result in exact accordance with the best rules known. Others will somehow succeed splendidly even though they may proceed in apparently direct opposition to all the accepted standards of practice.

The most important rule of all is to love and *know* your dog—and make sure that he loves and *knows* you. Strangers can accomplish but little in harmony. Almost any boy can teach whatever he wants to most any dog. The reason is that there is a sympathetic bond between them. There must be the closest possible similar bond between you and the dog you are attempting to teach to hunt for you in the field.

John S. Wise of Virginia wrote a great dog story called Diomed, more than thirty years ago. On page forty of that book he says: "I do not believe any man and dog can really know each other thoroughly unless they sleep together for some time."

Now it may not be necessary to go to quite this extreme—and I doubt if Mr. Wise meant to be taken too literally. But what he did want to convey is worth thinking about. Especially if you've been wondering why you aren't getting quite all that you think you should in the way of service from your Bird Dog. Get to *know him*. Give him a fair chance to *know you*. Then if to the knowing a touch of mutual love can be injected, you have the answer—and the whole answer—to most of your gun dog problems. For, as I have said, the fullest development is based upon intimacy and companionship, rather than merely mechanical processes. A baby, for instance, usually learns to talk without any special set lessons. The rudiments of grammar are taught later, and that's when refinement comes in. Dog development is a very similar process and I shall try to illustrate what I mean with some examples.

In these days of automobiles, a hunting dog

early comes into association with a car. This is necessary for transportation to fields where hunting may be indulged in. One of the first requirements, therefore, is to accustom a dog to an automobile. Many of them will become car sick at first—but the only cure for that is to keep taking them until they get over it. Most of them will get over it very quickly. Some may require more time.

When I open the door of my car to take the dogs out, the older ones hop right in. They would usually do so without any statement from me. If there were a young dog in the bunch, he would be apt to follow the older ones. However, when I open the car door for the dogs, I always accompany it by the invitation: "All right, get in." After a very few times a young dog thus adds to his vocabulary the knowledge of the meaning of that command. If you have a young dog which doesn't naturally follow the older ones, you will merely pick him up and put him in the car, and as you do so, say to him: "All right, get in." After two or three times he will be doing it of his own accord. You don't go to any special pains about the matter—but it is a lesson none the less. The command has been associated with the action. You have taught the dog something which will come in handy in many ways. You open the kennel door and use the same command —"Get in there." In the case of an intelligent dog, practically the same command may later be used to put him anywhere you want him to go, even though it may be down a steep ditch bank to retrieve a bird.

Regardless of what anyone else may say or believe, I know that just a natural intimacy with dogs will accomplish more than all the stilted methods of procedure in the world. That's why you hear some old hunters tell such marvelous stories of some of their old-time dogs. Seasons were longer then. There were seasons on more varieties of game. There was even spring shooting. Old hunters spent more time with their dogs as a rule than many of us do today. This developed the so-much-needed intimacy from constant companionship. There were few, if any, other sports such as golf, and the time some of us spend at this or other games was spent by the old-timers with their dogs. No wonder we hear of performances indicating highly developed intelligence!

A few nights ago we had a picnic supper on our screened porch at my home. Four of my dogs were playing in the backyard outside. One of them was a young setter of which I am very fond, and he wanted to come in on the porch with me. I let him in. He smelled the food. It was enticing. He stood by my chair and begged. Now a point I want to make is this—I had not yet taught this young dog to lie down or "charge" at command. He and I have, however, been very intimate. His training for actual hunting is pretty well finished. He is stanch on game and steady to shot and wing. He is ready to take on some of the refinements—but remember that I had never yet made any effort to teach him to "drop," "charge," or "lie down" (all three commands having the same object—it merely being necessary for each individual to select the command he prefers and use that same one constantly).

But while I had never taught this dog that particular command, I have taught him a great many other things. He knows that when

I give him an order it must be obeyed. He loves me and *wants* to obey. He and I have developed such an intimacy that he can pretty generally understand what I want whether he has heard the actual words before or not. Dogs talk to us, you know, almost entirely by actions. Since this is their language, they are naturally adept at interpreting sign language on our part—provided intimacy and confidence have been developed as an aid in the interpretation.

So as this young dog stood by my side at the table begging for food, I looked him straight in the eye, raising my hand palm out, and said: "Sam, lie down." He looked at me and I repeated the command in the same even tone of voice. As I did so I turned my hand slightly downward, accompanying the voice command by this motion of the hand. The dog dropped. I was delighted. He kept his head raised and looked at me inquiringly. He wondered what it was all about. He could interpret from my manifest satisfaction that he had done right. That pleased him. A dog always wants to do the right thing. When a dog doesn't do the right thing, it is, nine times out of ten, because the right thing hasn't been made clear to him or because his natural desire to do the right thing has been confused either by inefficient or unsympathetic development.

Now it is but natural that, after Sam acted on my command, he was ready to get up again pretty quickly. When I didn't say "All right," or give any other command to indicate permission, he thought he would try it on his own responsibility. Just as he started to get up, I pressed my hand firmly on his back and said: "Down, Sam"—and he dropped again. Then I looked at him and added two new words which he had not heard before: "Stay there." Before that meal was over I had taught the dog to "lie down" and to "stay there." There were two lessons rolled into one and it didn't even interfere with my meal. Most training (but not all training, I admit) is almost as easy as that—provided you have laid the foundation right. The trouble with so many of us is that we miss out in the all-important foundation. A man wrote me the other day that he had punished his dog because the dog wouldn't retrieve. It developed that he hadn't even taught the dog to retrieve. Therefore, the dog didn't know why he was being punished. What that man was actually doing was teaching the dog *not* to retrieve.

Suppose there had been any punishment connected with that little lesson I gave Sam the other night. He wouldn't have deserved any punishment—not even if he hadn't obeyed so well. Punishment should be administered for willful infraction of the known rules. It should never be administered for infraction of rules that are not known. Some six months from now, if I have occasion to order Sam to "lie down," after the lesson has been well drilled in the meantime, if he should then refuse he should be punished. That would drive home the fact that he *must* obey. Punishment in connection with that first lesson the other night would have destroyed his trust in me. With that destroyed, his value would be impaired.

A dog which is always expecting punishment—never quite sure when it is going to come, and never quite sure why it is being administered—that sort of a dog never amounts to much. And he isn't given a chance to amount to much. A dog without utter confidence in his master—which is a means of developing confidence in himself—will *never* amount to much in the hunting field. Whether it be pointer, setter, retriever or hound, the dog worth while is the one with enough confidence to strike out daringly on his own initiative—yet initiative which is always under the master's power to control.

No training can be successful without *thinking.* In the case of difficult dogs I have often lain awake at night trying to figure out ways and means for accomplishing the desired end—trying to figure out what could possibly be the mental processes of the dog which are obstructing my desires. To think things out is infinitely more important than to know all the rules in the world. I, therefore, urge and beg all of my readers to do more thinking. You can't do too much. *Study your dog.* I don't see how you can otherwise expect to handle him. I have never known a competent trainer who did not know that each dog requires special study.

H. L.

PROLOGUE

EDITOR'S NOTE—The following comment was written by Mr. Lytle especially for *The Saturday Evening Post* and was published by that magazine in their issue of Sept. 20, 1930. It is reprinted here by special permission of The Curtis Publishing Company.

Even such a short span as a hundred years is a long time in America. Consider, then, *five* hundred years—five centuries—a date more distant than the day Columbus sailed from Spanish shores on the voyage that ended with the discovery of a great new land.

Yet five centuries ago we have definite record of Bird Dogs in England. The old Spanish Pointer breed goes back still further into the dim records of antiquity. Some say this breed was used to put pointing instinct into the Setters when the latter were being "manufactured" with Spaniel blood as the fundamental basis.

All that was before the days of the "scatter," or shot, gun as we know it to-day. Hunters carried great nets which they threw over the birds as found by the dogs. Either

Pointers or Setters were used—but the records show that the latter breed found greatest favor, due to the fact that in those days these dogs dropped on point, or "set" their game. The net was thrown over the dog, as well as the birds in front of him, and the "setting" dog could be covered by the net with less danger of the prey having a chance to escape.

Later, with the advent of the scatter gun, the Setters were taught to stand erect on their points, so that the attitudes of both breeds "on game" became practically identical. With the use of a gun instead of a net the standing position was preferable because of the fact that a standing dog is much more readily seen than a crouching one.

It is strange how tradition travels. In spite of the fact that the Setters have been standing up on their points for several centuries, there are many people to-day who still believe that the difference between the Pointer and the Setter is that the former points standing while the latter points crouched. There also continue to exist even stranger misconceptions. Some of these are unique. About two years ago a man I know, who has hunted all his life, bred his Irish Setter bitch to an English Setter dog. That alone is not so unusual—it has been done before. If you want a cross-bred dog, this one is as good as any. It was, however, a very great lack of correct information that caused this man to think that in making this cross he was producing Gordon Setters!

The Gordon is the Setter breed of Scotland. It was created years and years ago by the Duke of Gordon. It has become as distinct a breed as either the English or the Irish Setter. The Irish-English cross no more produced Gordon Setters than would you get Irish Setters by crossing a Gordon with an English Setter. Many people believe there is a distinct breed of Setters known as Llewellins. Such is not the case. The name Llewellin refers to a certain *strain* of English Setters tracing back to a common ancestry. Thus it is but a strain of breeding—not a breed. All Llewellins are English Setters. Only a very rare few could confirm a Llewellin pedigree if they'd see it. Yet pedigree is the only basis for qualification. Some people think it's a matter of markings or color. How wrong they are!

Other misconceptions are prevalent. A little while ago I was asked to speak before a prominent noontide club on the subject of Bird Dogs. Those present seemed quite interested and after the meeting a number came up to ask special questions. "Is it true," one man inquired, "that a Bird Dog gets into such a highly nervous state when pointing game that he often bleeds at the tip of his tail?" Now, manifestly, such is not the case. It is true, however, that a Bird Dog's tail will often bleed when he is at work in the field. Constant switching against thorns and briars is the cause. Many dogs carry "merry" tails while hunting—which is a very much sought for trait—and these are especially apt to develop a mighty sore caudal appendage, unless the member is taped to protect it. Thus it is briars that have caused the bleeding—not the dog's nervous excitement on point. It is, however, nervous excitement which causes *style* on point.

It scarcely seems necessary, but perhaps might not be amiss to explain that a Bird

PROLOGUE

Dog (either Pointer or Setter) shows the presence of game by "pointing," motionless, in the direction from whence comes the scent that warns him of unseen birds. The hunter is thus "told" to get ready. The dog's attitude also indicates just about the spot from which the birds may be expected to flush. If the hunter is experienced, he may pretty accurately determine in advance the probable direction of flight. Position from which flushed and location of the nearest cover are the governing factors. That the birds sometimes break the rules of expectation simply adds zest to the sport.

The truly well-finished dog will remain steady to wing and shot. That is, he will continue to stand steady when the game is flushed—and even after the shot is fired. If a bird falls to the gun, he still should not move until ordered on to retrieve. There are a number of refinements which the art of training may add—but these are the fundamentals.

In the early days of this country—when Daniel Webster shot over his Setters, for instance—and still to-day in England—game was so abundant that finding it presented almost no problem at all. A hunter even without a dog could find more than enough. Varying degrees of dog aptitude involved little more than *manners in handling game.* The ability to *find* game was of lesser importance. In other words, *training* was *everything.* Thus the ability of handler or trainer was of more concern than any ability the dog might have. One canine might differ from another in degree of *finish;* but natural ability came only slightly into account. With the exception of the quality of *nose,* not much else was called for—not when game was so abundantly plentiful. Merely finding game was child's play, for game was everywhere. In those days a hunter walked through a field and his dogs "quartered" the cover systematically in front of him. It was methodically mechanical.

But the years sped on, as the years have a way of doing. Came a time, at last, when game grew scarcer. And as this condition increased, a premium was put on the dog that proved the best *searcher* and *finder.* Nose alone ceased to be enough. Gradually hunters came to appreciate a dog's manifest *intelligence* in searching. The finish shown in handling game must be coupled to the ability to *find* game to be handled. The old plan of methodical quartering finally gave way to the idea of giving the dog more right to use his head; of depending more and more upon him to show "bird sense," initiative, and good judgment in hunting. Yet, with it all, he must still maintain contact with his handler. Not all cover contained game, so we began to ask our dogs to pass up unlikely and go directly to likely-looking cover. This saved a lot of lost time, and time is important. Hunting days are all too short. Dogs with the *brains* to search intelligently came into demand. Another factor began to count more than ever before—and that factor was *courage*. As Bird Dogs were asked to cover more ground more quickly, it took stamina plus *courage* to go the route of a hard day afield.

In 1874 near Memphis, Tennessee, came the first public competition for Bird Dogs ever held in America. The sport had taken root in England a few years earlier. Such competitions are known as *field trials.* Growth of interest has been steady. To-day in this country we have some two hundred regularly functioning clubs sponsoring in the neighborhood of three hundred or more field trial fixtures annually. There are several circuits, beginning on the prairies of Saskatchewan in early September and swinging on southward as the frost hits the pumpkin in other localities. The feathered game on which the trials are run include prairie chicken, the ruffed grouse, the quail, the pheasant and the Hungarian partridge. The most coveted title of all is the National Championship run each winter on quail near Grand Junction, Tennessee.

Conceptions have continued to change. Early judges scored the competing dogs on a scale of credits for each phase of performance. From this credit or "point system" we developed the "heat system"; and from out of the experience of these two earlier systems came the "spotting system" of to-day. The competing dogs are braced together in pairs, according as their names are drawn from slips in a hat. In the first series each brace is hunted for the same definite and equal length of time. It is usually left to the discretion of the judges whether or not a second series is needed to determine the winners.

Field trials brought a broader and deeper interest in Bird Dogs than ever before. The best blood of England was imported, and the "blue bloods," after many and exhaustive tests, proved superior to our native "cold-blooded" dogs—just as thoroughbred race horses have similarly proved their supremacy. Blue-blooded stock led to an interest in breeding and a study of the importance of blood lines. Particularity as to pedigree led to stud books and truly authentic registration. The Field Dog Stud Book at Chicago features Bird Dogs, but registers other breeds also.

With the growth of field trials another factor came into play in the canine world as pertaining to Bird Dogs. Whereas hunters had always been intimate with a few dogs of their own—and perhaps also the relatively few owned by their own hunting cronies—opportunity was now multiplied many times to see and to know what the best sort of performance can be. Conceptions were thus lifted from out of their former narrow limits and broader vision was the result.

This closer study of dogs revealed much. And a closer study of game itself followed upon the heels of the former. The results have been amazingly beneficial. To the old, narrow, and limited conceptions of Bird Dog performance has come an appreciation of what we now call "class," which involves speed, range, intelligence and judgment, animation, style, nose, courage, and endurance —all coupled to the climax of perfect manners on game. Don't you see how the factors of appreciation have multiplied?

The perpetually growing fraternity of field trial enthusiasts is becoming constantly keener for the sport we love so well. This boundless enthusiasm has given *the greatest impetus yet known to the cause of game restoration.* And who can doubt that game does need restoring in America!

We must have game in the field for the Bird Dogs to find and to point—or field trials cannot go on. Field trial fans all realize this, and they constitute as a body the deepest students, the most determined workers, and the most enthusiastic supporters of all game restoration movements. As pertaining to upland game in particular, this will be found incontrovertibly true.

Live birds are the standard of value in the field trials, whereas in the game bag it is only the dead bird that counts. This has a very important bearing on the matter. Recruits to the field trial fraternity all come from the ranks of the hunting field. This is but natural and could not be otherwise. It simply means that all such hunters are getting a higher conception than merely to kill. Most field trialers continue also to remain hunters —but they have a higher and a deeper appreciation of it all. And this can have naught but a beneficial influence. The *quality of the dog's performance becomes what counts*—not merely the frequency of the kill.

There is another interesting feature to consider. While field trialers continue to remain hunters, their period for pleasure afield is tremendously lengthened. Hunting seasons and bag limits have been constantly constricted. The hunter who does not indulge also in the competitions now has a mighty short season each year in most states to indulge his favorite pastime. But there is no closed season on merely flushing live birds—and there is no bag limit on such harmless flushing. And a fellow who is preparing his dog for a field trial has plenty of *incentive.* Without such incentive there would be much less fun. But a field trial trophy will be remembered and prized long after a dead bird is eaten and forgotten. In a nutshell, field trial fans are working and enjoying their dogs eight months of the year. No hunting season is that long! Dogs should not be taken afield during the nesting season, but training can begin in August and run into early April.

The incentive for more and longer work with dogs results in greater knowledge of them. Such knowledge, as it broadens, leads to greater appreciation of *quality* in a dog's work. Thus the source of true pleasure shifts—coming from the good work your dog does, rather than from the good shot you make. Those who merely hunt in open season must drink their only cup of joy based on *kills.* But field trials bring enlarged opportunity for even a keener joy based on *thrills.*

The Bird Dogs of to-day are better than they ever were—and there are more of them. They must be better for they're bred to be —and breeding is known to count. It counts in cattle, horses, poultry—and it counts in dogs. There are still poor Bird Dogs, of course, as there always have been and always will be—but the average has been raised, and all is well.

CHAPTER I

YOUR POINTER OR SETTER PUPPY

THE logical place to start our discussion seems to be at the very beginning. Suppose we consider the puppy, and then bring him along gradually through his various stages of development. That, in short, is the plan we have in mind.

While our main comments shall be directed particularly to the Bird Dog puppy (Pointer or Setter), yet many of the underlying fundamentals will apply equally to the Spaniel, Hound, Griffin, Chesapeake Bay dog, or other breeds that may be used by men in connection with sports afield or astream.

The puppy comes naturally into the picture for consideration. It is the puppies of to-day which are destined to become the working dogs of to-morrow—just as our sons are destined to become the sportsmen of to-morrow. Therefore, the development of the youngsters is a problem that is constantly with us. The faithful old dog may have seen his last season; or the day will certainly dawn when such shall come to pass. Furthermore, in the case of the Pointer or Setter, it is a mighty wise sportsman who sees himself re-enforced with a fresh dog to divide up the work. So, from any standpoint, the puppy seems to be the logical starting point for discussion.

This is especially true for those who may be thinking of a field trial prospect. Puppies whelped from January 1st through April of any year are the proper age to start in the Puppy Stakes a year later and in the Derby Stakes two years hence. Our main consideration in these pages, however, shall be the gun dog from the standpoint of comrade and helper in the hunting fields.

There are several considerations relative to securing the puppy. Will you breed him or buy him? If you own an unregistered bitch, don't breed her. Do not perpetuate an unknown strain. If she is registered, you will derive a great deal of pleasure from "raising your own." In that case, there is a certain intimacy of interest that cannot be secured in any other manner. But let me especially inject a word of suggestion here. As the sire of your puppies, don't select some local dog merely because of the erroneous conception that "cheapness recommends it." Cheapness is a poor recommendation in this case. You will learn this when you come to offer for sale the extra puppies that you do not care to keep. The dog buying public doesn't readily fall for the unknown quantity. If you breed to an unknown sire, you will find that (1) your puppies will be harder to sell; and (2) you can't get the price for them. The fact that they are harder to sell means that it will take you longer to sell them—both of which conditions involve expense that cuts down your profit. And the fact that you may have to sell them at a sacrifice price reduces any possible profit still further.

Cheap stud fees are bound to mean cheap puppies. Cheap stud fees may also mean too many puppies for the market—and the natural law of supply and demand cuts quite a figure here. The governing idea in all breeding should be quality rather than quantity. Quality breeding is bound by the natural law of such things to lead toward more profitable prices all down the line—better prices for grown stock; for puppies; and for stud service. Furthermore, that logically leads to a higher class of dogs all through the breeds.

So the proven plan that is always best, and which is cheapest in the long run—with the best chance, also, of giving you what you want—is to select for your mating a stud dog of known reputation and merit, a dog which has proven himself both in the field and as a sire. You will some day have cause to thank me for this suggestion if you follow it. And you will have the further satisfaction that comes from contributing to the building up of families—as against indiscriminate and promiscuous breeding.

Many of you, however, and perhaps the majority, will be in the position of having to buy a puppy rather than breed one. Even in that case, the same fundamentals hold true. Beware of the puppy that is offered too cheap. He hasn't the same chance of proving desirable in the end—and hence may prove more expensive than the puppy which represents a more normal initial investment. The reason for this is that you may not get a sure line on his merits until after you have spent a considerable amount of time and money on him. Then, if he proves to be a disappointment, a whole season of satisfaction may be lost—not to mention the possible expense involved. So it pays to select a puppy from known parents—and there should be a performance record on each side of the family tree. Too many persons pin all their faith on the sire, forgetting that the dam of the litter contributes at least equally to the qualities that the puppies are to inherit. Therefore, make it a point to learn just as much about the mother as you do about the sire of the puppy you are buying.

Don't ever buy a puppy younger than two months of age; and don't buy one younger than from three to four months if he is to be shipped very far. A long train trip can easily throw a young puppy all out of fix. In that case you may have difficulty bringing him back to normal—if you *ever* do. Therefore, never take one away from its mother younger than two months—while from four to six months will always be a safer age.

Above all, be sure that your puppy is actually eligible to registration. In this connection, confusion will sometimes arise in the case of those whose experience is limited. It is not enough that you just get the "papers." You must know that those papers certify the certainty of registration. Some of you may think now that you don't care—but, as sure as the sun will set to-night, you will live to regret it if your dog is not registered in one of the stud books, and particularly the one which makes a specialty of the Bird Dog breeds.

Not long ago, I had occasion to see it take ten years for an old hunter to regret the fact that his dog had never been registered. He had a splendid Pointer, but the papers had never been secured from the man who bred him and my friend had never paid much attention to it anyhow, thinking that he didn't care. A little later the breeder died and the opportunity was gone. As the years went on, this fine Pointer won his way more surely all the time into the heart of his owner. When the dog had reached ten years of age, my friend realized that his days were becoming numbered, and became obsessed with the idea of perpetuating the blood and securing for himself a puppy sired by the old dog, with which to carry on. He was, however, justly anxious that the dam of this contemplated litter be equal to the occasion, and he approached me on the subject of a mating with a Pointer bitch of mine. I turned him down flatly. I could not afford to sacrifice my registered bitch to such a litter and frankly told him so. For ten years this man had gone on blissfully content—but he saw the day when he had lived to regret bitterly that his favorite Pointer's blood could not be carried on. To make up for my apparent brutality in refusing the mating, I made him a present of a registered puppy and I don't believe my friend will ever again have one that isn't.

You, too, will live to know the day of regret if you are careless in your belief regarding this matter of whether or not your puppy is eligible to registration. The regret may come early, or it may come late. And, the later it comes, the keener the regret will be. Therefore, since manifestly the important thing is to *get started* right, we have begun our suggestions by covering these important thoughts in connection with the acquisition of the prospect. If we are agreed on these important fundamentals, we are then in a position to go ahead and discuss the various steps in the development of the puppy in their relative order.

Just one final word: If you have field trial aspirations, buy a puppy whelped as early as possible after the first of the new year. Puppies whelped later than April suffer a severe handicap in Puppy Stakes, and later as Derbies, because they have to give away too much advantage in both age and experience.

CHAPTER II

SOME SUGGESTIONS ON FEEDING

FEEDING is always an important consideration. The real young puppy should be fed three or four times a day and not too much at a time. It is vital to feed often rather than to attempt a stuffing process in fewer meals. Young stomachs can't handle too much at a time without disastrous effects. During the first month or so, the mother's care and nursing are all that is required. At about five weeks of age it is advisable to help nature along by starting to teach the puppies to lap a little lukewarm milk from a bowl on their own responsibility. By gently dipping their little noses in the milk, and letting them lick it off, one or several puppies from a litter will be found that will take to it naturally. These will quickly teach the more reluctant ones and the process will afford a great relief to the already overtaxed mother.

There was a time when puppies were weaned abruptly; but the present plan is a more gradual one. During this gradual weaning process, it is advisable to start with just one helpful feeding a day, increasing as the mother becomes more reluctant and more unable to care for the puppies on her own responsibility. By the time she weans them entirely, the outside feeding should be increased to four times a day. This should be maintained up to the time the puppies are four or five months old, according to the way they are thriving, and in consultation with your veterinarian.

At four or five months of age, the tapering down process begins and the puppies may be fed gradually a little more at a time, and less often. Three meals a day (still not stuffing them at any one meal) is a good average from four up to six or eight months of age. From eight months up to a year or a year and a half, the feeding may be twice a day, morning and evening. From a year and a half on, your then practically grown dog should thrive on one good meal a day, preferably in the evening. So long as he relishes his food and licks the pan clean, he may have at this age all he cares to eat. Never try to force him to eat more than he wants, because a grown dog knows better than you do how much it is best for him to have. The healthiest kind of a sign is when he licks the pan clean, still willing to take a little more. However, there will always be some dogs that are dainty feeders. If this is just the dog's natural tendency, there is no cause for alarm.

There is nothing better than table scraps, when these are available. The average size family will usually leave enough for one or two dogs. Those who keep more dogs will find it necessary to use other foods. In feeding table scraps, always be careful to eliminate chicken bones or others of a similar sharp, brittle character. Perhaps it is just as well to eliminate potatoes until after a puppy is anywhere from eight to ten months old. After that, potatoes are really a very good food—all previous opinions to the contrary notwithstanding.

Dry (but not stale) bread soaked with milk is excellent for the young puppy. Vegetables are very important, especially during the warmer months of spring and summer. Tomatoes are splendid and should be mixed with greens such as beet tops or spinach. Cabbage and onions are very good and dogs will eat them when blended in with other foods. It is naturally to be understood that the puppy might refuse any of these if offered separately—but he will relish them when mixed in reasonable proportions with his porridge.

Hamburger cooked with oatmeal is good when the weather is cool; while rice may be substituted for the oatmeal when the days grow warmer. Various combinations cooked up with corn meal are also fine to hunt on in winter—though too heating for a summer diet. There are various biscuits on the market that are splendid to use from once a day to several times a week. Some dogs are finicky about biscuits, especially after they have been educated to other foods, but some kind of biscuit can usually be found that any dog will relish. Your dogs may prefer one make and my dogs another. A little experimenting will soon indicate what brand of biscuit your dogs will accept.

But don't forget that the dog is naturally a carnivorous animal and requires meat—which should always be the basis of canine diet. There are a number of excellent balanced rations on the market, blending meat, cereals and vegetables in proper proportions with cod liver oil and other ingredients. Many of these are very reliable products that come in cans, ready to serve, and which any dog in the world will relish. These foods are most convenient to use, whether at home or on a hunt. In the latter case, they are especially useful, for you simply count your dogs and the number of days you expect to be hunting, and match this total by taking the necessary number of cans. Then add a can opener to your equipment and your feeding problem is solved.

In the above connection allow me to say that, while one good meal a day is sufficient for most dogs of mature age, when inactive, I do not regard one meal a day as enough for a dog to hunt on. Perhaps the easiest and best thing to feed in the morning (because it is a condensed food and hence not bulky) is a one-pound can of balanced ration to each dog. At noon be fair enough to share a bit of your own lunch with your canine companions. Chances are they'll have earned it as much as you have. At night give the dogs a good substantial meal. More canned food will do in a pinch; but for variety I like to change off with corn bread and a general run of meat and other table scraps whenever possible. Shredded Wheat is a wonderful dog food, mixed either with soup, milk, vegetables or hamburger. Raw eggs mixed with Shredded Wheat are also good and have great strength-building value.

The problem of worms is often a serious one with puppies. However, I would like to inject a word of caution here. I believe that a young puppy should be wormed oftener and not too strenuously at a time, just as he should be fed oftener and not too much at a time. In a grown dog it may be advisable to "knock" the worms pretty much with one dose. Don't try that with a puppy! An overdose of vermifuge can kill as quick and as dead as the worms. If you consult a veterinarian in the matter of worming your puppy (and I believe you should), make sure that he is one who is in sympathy with light worming for puppies. Otherwise look up someone else. You've got to watch for, and keep fighting worms all the time—but a knock-out blow in the case of such a fight is not the desirable end. Unless it is the puppy that you want to knock out!

While meat, being the natural diet for a dog, should be the basis of all feeding, and may be fed all the year round, less should be used in the summer than at other seasons. Greens and other vegetables should be utilized. Beet tops, cabbage, onions, and tomatoes—are all fine foods. A dog will eat any or all of these if mixed up appetizingly with a little meat to give the dish the right "doggy" flavor.

It is always well, however, to find some make of dog biscuit that your dogs will eat and have such biscuits available to feed either dry or softened in milk. Bread and milk, or crackers and milk, make a good feed to use once or twice a week—but use dry bread and not fresh bread. It doesn't make any difference how hard and dry the bread may be if it is not moldy. The milk will soften it up and the dog will be all the better for it.

Distemper

The greatest menace ahead of the puppy is that of distemper. I know of one man who, when he buys puppies, always asks the seller to name his price. Then my friend counters with the proposal to pay one-half that amount on delivery—which constitutes a paid-up sale if the puppy dies from distemper. The agreement is, however, that if the puppy lives through distemper, my friend is then to pay the balance plus fifty per cent additional. Thus the seller gets only half his price if the puppy dies; but he gets half again above his selling price if the puppy lives. It isn't a bad idea.

I have one dog that has reached six years of age and has never had distemper to my knowledge. It is claimed that the triple National Champion, Becky Broomhill, never had it. But such examples are far too rare —and distemper is always ahead of you, unless it is behind you. This is especially true in the case of gun dogs, which are by necessity constantly thrown with other dogs, either in the course of a hunt or in connection with field trial competitions.

There are various distemper inoculations of more or less value. Some experienced dog men don't try to fight it at all. Long experience has taught them that it is too discouraging! These just let their dogs go through it, for better or for worse. They feel they are just so much ahead in the case of whatever number of puppies may be left alive.

Personally, I don't like to give up any kind of a fight—without making a fight out of it. The weather has a good deal to do with your success in fighting distemper. Fresh air and sunshine are the best cures in the world. Above all, keep your puppy *dry*. That is half the battle. Bright, summery days are the best—but even the cold of winter, if you can keep the puppy dry, is better than damp though warmer weather.

It is especially important to keep the puppy eating. If the distemper is a light case, this may not be so hard. But in bad cases you have a real problem. Force feeding is then necessary—and raw eggs represent the easiest and best solution in force feeding.

While the curse of distemper lays its devastating hands heavily upon all branches of the canine families, it is undoubtedly true that it reaches its peak as a scourge among the gun dogs. The reason for this is simply that gun dogs have more opportunity for coming in contact with the disease due to the fact that they are constantly traveling about from place to place in connection either with field trials or actual hunting. Many breeds live more isolated lives, except when exhibited at bench shows, and that is the reason why we, to whom our gun dogs mean so much, have more to fear from distemper than most other fanciers. Perhaps, too, this may have had something to do with the fact that two gun dog men have occupied the highest offices in the American Distemper Committee.

At this writing, the English Distemper Committee, which is the parent body, has recently issued a report through the American Committee that a point has now been reached where it is possible to say that the means has been found of preventing the disease of distemper. Ask your Veterinarian for the latest word on this. Perhaps much of the former peril of this dread disease may have been removed by the time this book is off the press.

CHAPTER III

CARE OF THE DOG

THE summer months are a time when special care must be exerted to keep your gun dogs comfortable. The days of our dreams are those "when the frost is on the pumpkin." But the hot summer months must be endured —by both man and dog—and it is up to each of us to keep our canine companions as clean and cool as we can.

Fleas will bother him (or her) almost to distraction unless you do something about it to help with relief. Fleas are about as annoying as anything with which a dog has to contend. It seems almost impossible to get rid of them completely. We can, however, keep fighting them all the while and reduce the grievance to a minimum. The dog's kennel or sleeping quarters should be disinfected at least once a week and preferably oftener. It won't take long and the results are worth while. The dog will appreciate it and so will you in the long run. The regular use of a good disinfectant is not an encouragement to fleas; but more important still is the fact that the hot months are when dogs are most susceptible to skin troubles, such as mange, and an ounce of prevention is worth a pound of cure. Keep the sleeping quarters, and the entire kennel, as sweet and clean as possible.

Red Cedar shavings are a great discouragement to fleas and may be secured from a number of sources. The advertising columns of sport magazines often carry messages of firms offering such shavings for sale at a reasonable price. A dog whose summer bed is made in Cedar shavings will not have occasion to get most of his exercise scratching.

A sulphur dip is an excellent thing, not only to carry off fleas, but also to destroy the germs that lead to skin troubles in the summer months. The present writer believes that one reason why skin troubles are so prevalent in summer is because most dogs are scratching fleas so constantly that their skin is irritated by their claws and that paves the way for any little infection to take hold. The following is an approved formula for a home-made sulphur dip and it is recommended to those who would be fair to their dogs in the hot months:

1 can Lewis' Lye

5 lbs. flour sulphur (Atomic sulphur mixes better)

4 bars soap

40 gallons soft water (rain water is best)

Mixing

Bring about eight or ten gallons of the water to a boil, then add one can of Lewis' Lye and sulphur, boiling gently for one full hour, stirring constantly to prevent sulphur sticking to the container and scorching.

Pour the mixture into a 50-gallon barrel. Then chip up the soap and dissolve in a bucket of hot water and add to the batch, filling the barrel up to within eight or ten inches of the top with clear water.

After cooling, the dip is ready for use.

Dip the dogs every week or ten days to keep vermin under control—twice a week is recommended at first in bad cases.

Applying the Dip

Grasp both hind feet with the left hand, pass right hand under the body and grab the left foreleg. Lift dog up and lower gently into the barrel, hind quarters first, then slip left hand up and grasp front legs with right hand under muzzle. Immerse up to the roots of the ears, being careful not to get solution in eyes or ears.

It is a very wise precaution to have a good sulphur dip preparation constantly on hand during the summer months. It fights fleas, is a preventive against skin troubles, and is a relief to the dogs.

Any good flea soap will knock vast numbers of these irritating insects, especially if plenty of time and elbow grease are used in the application. If you just give the dog a lick and a promise, however, even the best of flea soaps will fail to accomplish their purpose, especially with a long-haired dog. A Setter, for example, will have to be given more of a bath than a Pointer, if you are to accomplish the same results in the way of ridding him of fleas. The dog's coat must be wet clear through and the lather worked vigorously right into the pores of the skin. If you only touch the surface, the fleas will be underneath undisturbed and hiding like so many quail in good cover. A good bath once a week in the summer is not too often; and a good plan, in order to be sure to have enough water to accomplish a real wetting, is to take the dog to a little creek or stream and let him stand about ankle deep in the water while you wade in barefooted with your cake of flea soap and go to work. When you have worked in the soap until your arms get tired, you can just lead the dog out to a little deeper water for a good rinsing. In winter, the dog need not be bathed at all; but brushing out his coat regularly with a stiff brush will do him a world of good—stirs up his circulation and makes him *feel better* as well as look better.

And speaking of water in connection with the bath, let's not overlook the importance of water from the standpoint of drinking. A dog's water pan should always be kept filled with fresh water at all seasons of the year, but at no time is this so vital in importance as during the heat of summer. Fresh water in his pan once a day may suffice in the cooler months—but once a day is not often enough during June, July and August. Just imagine yourself having a pitcher of fresh water poured for you in the morning and then being asked to quench your thirst from that same pitcher of the same water all during the rest of a hot day! Well, if that wouldn't satisfy you, it won't satisfy the dog either—and if it isn't good enough for you, neither is it good enough for him. I'll tell you another thing—and I don't dream it—neither do I merely think it—but I *know* it. I know that these little courtesies, which dogs so much appreciate, breed something deeper in the way of contact between you that will lead to a more faithful service in the field in the fall. All I hope is that readers will not take this statement too lightly. I *know* what I am talking about. And I am not referring to just water alone—but I am referring to all manner of little intimacies that gear you and your dog closer together in many ways. These things lead to a greater love; to a greater understanding; and to a greater service.

Let me also add a few words about your dog's bed. We have already mentioned the use of Red Cedar shavings for the bed in summer as a protection against fleas. If these shavings are fine enough, a dog can actually make his bed in them. If those you get are too rough for that purpose, they may simply be strewn about the kennel and in the run way. It is also possible to make a little mattress with the Cedar shavings as a filler. Straw, however, should *not* be used for a dog's bedding in the summer time. Oats straw should *never be used* at any time. Any tendency toward skin trouble seems to be especially aggravated by oats straw. In winter, wheat straw makes a very good bedding, particularly in view of its warmth if enough of it is used to give the dog a chance to curl up in it. When the writer uses wheat straw in winter, he piles it in about two feet deep and dogs certainly relish the protection therefrom during cold nights. But straw at any time of year *should be changed often;* and you must also guard against dampness. The great need for a dog's bed is that it shall be dry. The bottom of a straw bed will get damp in time and that should never be allowed to occur.

A fine summer bed for dogs is to have a

rectangular iron framework made with legs that raise it three or four inches from the ground. In other words, make a regular little iron bed of a dimension that will comfortably accommodate the size of whatever dog you own. Over the top of this iron framework stretch a closely meshed wire sufficiently heavy to bear the weight of your dog. Fasten this netting securely all the way around so that it will not sag too much. You want it to sag some, and it naturally will, adding a degree of comfort. Get two pieces of the heaviest canvas, each piece somewhat larger than the actual dimensions of the bed. Lay this canvas covering over the bed and it is ready for use. The canvas may be tied on or simply laid on loose. The only disadvantage in tying it is that this may have a tendency to cause you to neglect changing it—and that brings up the reason why we suggested two of these canvas mats. Use one mat for two or three days. Then turn it over and use the other side. After that, take off that mat and use the other one in the same way. The canvas that is removed should be thoroughly disinfected and then hung up in the sun until again ready for use. Rain won't hurt it—and neither will the sun. Sun is an excellent disinfectant in itself. By interchanging the canvas in the way we have suggested, you will be pretty apt to eliminate skin troubles and the construction of the bed itself is exceptionally sanitary.

You wouldn't like to spend all your time on a hot day exposed to the summer sun. See that your dog has shade. You will always notice cattle or horses in the fields standing under some shade tree; and what they seek in this respect, your dog seeks also. Do not deny him that comfort.

For winter protection, see that the dog's sleeping quarters are as snug as possible—free from drafts. He can stand a lot of cold—if dry—and if accustomed to it. Do not keep him one night where it is warm and the next night where it is cold. Decide on one place or another—then don't change. Above all, be sure it is dry and not drafty.

So many people are really almost total strangers to their Bird Dogs! And so many Bird Dogs are really total strangers to their masters! No dog ever gives his best for a stranger; and no master ever gets the best from a stranger. You can't expect to be a stranger to your dog for eleven months of the year and then suddenly get on intimate working terms in a couple of weeks. It just isn't in the wood. Think over all the stories you have ever heard of greatness in dogs. I challenge anyone to report an authentic case of any dog ever showing the kind of service that amounts almost to genius, for a stranger. The writer would hazard the belief that back of every authentic tale of true canine greatness there can be uncovered a basis for that greatness in the form of a deep and abiding confidence between dog and master which has been nurtured and cultivated in a great common purpose and has led to a development of understanding and brain power on the part of the canine companion that has made possible the understanding of what is wanted and the accomplishment of real achievement.

Children start with no knowledge and are taught to develop their capacities. The development of a dog is exactly similar within certain limitations. Bear in mind that your dog cannot speak with you—except by manifestations. Yet in spite of the handicap of muteness, many of them understand far more than we realize. It is marvelous when we consider how much they can learn and how much they can do in spite of being denied the use of language.

As between dogs and children, bear in mind another thing. A child is still a child at twelve or fourteen years of age—yet in that many years a dog has lived his entire span of life and is usually past all usefulness. In those few short years he has gone through babyhood, childhood, middle age and maturity. At fourteen years of age a child's life is still all before him and his future has not yet even begun to unfold itself. Yet in those same few years a dog's life is all but spent. Into a comparatively few seasons must be crowded all they can ever hope to learn. Think that over! Isn't it marvelous, then, that they learn so much! And let me but merely add that in the case of those dogs that have failed to learn much by the time they have reached maturity, the blame can usually be found to lie at the door of an unappreciative and unsympathetic master. I have seen too many cases of development from nothing to true canine greatness not to know that this is true.

A friend of mine was recently telling me about his Pointer dog. He said the dog made friends with everyone—the butcher, the baker, the candlestick maker. He said he had never known anyone who came around his house with whom the dog was not willing to make friends. He added that he had never even heard his dog growl at a human being.

Yet he was awakened about two o'clock one morning by the most vicious actions on the part of this dog, which was chained in the yard. It developed that burglars were trying to enter the residence and the dog was trying to get at them. As it was, he wakened the family and the invaders were frightened away. In relating the circumstances to me, my friend expressed considerable surprise and wondered if the dog could have realized the difference between these "visitors" and others.

Why, of course, the dog realized the difference! He *knew.* And I know that he knew. There is nothing unbelievable about it at all. It is not even unusual for a dog to have such powers of discrimination.

CHAPTER IV

HOUSE BREAKING AND TEACHING TO "HEEL"

WHETHER you plan to keep your puppy indoors or out (the latter being where the working dogs will always thrive better) you will find it a wise precaution to make sure that he or she is house broken. On some hunting trip, or other occasion, the time may come when the wisdom of this will be well proven.

House breaking is not hard. I always do it naturally—and then it becomes especially simple. By nature the dog is clean. He becomes otherwise only from necessity. Don't make it necessary—and *there you have the answer.*

Whenever I want to house break a dog or puppy, I note the time of taking indoors. Then I never let the puppy wander about—but make him or her lie down. Thus can you watch them. At any sign of restlessness that you feel is caused by the need of relief, call the pupil quickly outside—and you stay there with him until the mission has been accomplished. Then immediately return indoors with the pupil. He will shortly come to realize that you are there to see that he may get outside when it is necessary; and it won't be very long before, as occasions arise, he will be coming to you with signs that will indicate his desire. And there will later come a time when he will not for worlds relieve himself unless you, or someone, are there to grant his unspoken requests.

We have mentioned watching for signs of restlessness. There may be cases where the pupil will give no such advance warnings. But he will suddenly make a "bee line" for relief. You must beat him to it—and hurry with him to the door. What follows is the same as before. If on any such occasions you fail to get to him in time, you simply follow the old-time process of rubbing his nose in it. Then take him outside for a while.

But in such cases as this, if you have kept him inside too long, the fault lies with you and not with the puppy. Be careful not to punish your pupil for your errors. He'll know and resent it. And he will be just that much harder to teach other things. Therefore, be careful and never keep the pupil inside too long, whether he shows any "signs" or not. When he has been in so long that you think he might have to go, take him outside even without the "signs." The process is the same—for it's dollars to doughnuts that he'll do something; in which case take him on back inside.

My own dogs are taught everything, from house breaking to field work, in the natural course of events. Like Topsy, they "just grow into it." There are mighty few, if any, set lessons—and fewer all the time. We just take the different situations in the natural course of events, as they arise, and settle the proper procedure then and there. We show what we want done when there is evident a manifest reason for doing exactly what we want to accomplish. Thus are the lessons driven home harder than otherwise. But this calls for understanding between pupil and teacher, based upon a companionship that has awakened love and developed confidence. As we get better acquainted, discussing these things through the pages that follow, you will become more than well aware of my beliefs and practices.

Teaching to "Heel"

Procure a very light, willowy switch. Call the dog to your side and start for a walk. He may want to run and play. Call him in to you and command him to "heel." He will not at first understand and will try to break on ahead at the first opportunity. Repeat the command to come back and to "heel." The next time he starts away, be prompt to order him back. Keep repeating the procedure until he understands that he must remain with you. Practice makes perfect. Keep at it—and you will accomplish the result in an unbelievably short time.

But you want the dog to remain at "heel" —not merely with you. Begin to push him back of you when he forges up even. Say "heel"—and *indicate* what you mean. Dogs grasp things *so* easily from the proper *signs.* They cannot understand word commands, you know, until certain words have been *taught* them. Teach them to associate words with manifestations or signs.

If by this time the dog is hard to keep in place behind you, flick him with the switch. Don't whip him—just "flick" him. *There is a difference.* The whip will cause him to snap back into position quickly. When you have him to this point of understanding, continue to carry the light switch for a while. Every time he gets overanxious and pulls up even, or ahead, flick him lightly and order to "heel." Before very long you won't need the help of the switch at all. The command alone will be all-sufficient.

Remember always that "circumstances alter cases." Study your individual dog and be governed accordingly. Try to get the "feel" of the art of handling—just as you try to get the proper "feel" of a golf club. Don't handle each and every dog the same way, regardless. They are as individual as we humans are. Handlers must learn this—else they'll fail as handlers. I have one dog I never even attempted to teach to "heel" for several seasons—that was her trouble! She never got far enough *away* from my heels. I did not want to encourage that failing. All my efforts with that individual were spent trying to get her to *go out.* That was the big job—but she finally rewarded all my efforts. Then—but not until then—it was time enough to teach her to "heel."

On the other hand, with a pupil of the opposite type—one of the bold goers that are hard ever to keep in—the sooner you teach them to "heel" the better off you may be. In this case, the lessons might be begun most any time after six months.

CHAPTER V

THE BIRD DOG BREEDS

EVEN among those who hunt, and often among those who have hunted all their lives, I have been surprised to find a tremendous lack of definite and assured information as pertaining to the different breeds of Bird Dogs, that is, the Irish, English and Gordon Setters, and the Pointers.

I know a man who has hunted all of his life; who has hunted in all parts of the country; who has hunted the grouse as well as the quail and the prairie chicken; and who has always owned Bird Dogs to hunt over; but who recently proved an astonishing lack of information with reference to the Bird Dog breeds.

This man owned an excellent Irish Setter bitch, which it just so happened he had purchased from me. I didn't hear anything about either him or her for a year or so, and then one day I got a letter suggesting that I come up to see his puppies. I called him long distance and asked what he had bred to —and he told me he had bred to a very good English Setter.

"Thus you see," he said, "my puppies are Gordon Setters!" I could scarcely believe my ears. I wrote him explaining that the cross of an Irish Setter with an English Setter would not produce a Gordon Setter. He then phoned me about it—and finally came down to see me. It was quite some time before I could convince him that he was really wrong.

The Gordon Setter is the Bird Dog of Scotland. Credit for the origin of the breed is given to the Duke of Gordon. Gordon Setters are always black with tan trimmings; but a dog that is merely black and tan is not necessarily a Gordon Setter. A Gordon is just as distinct a breed as the Pointer is a distinct breed. Yet I found that my friend had got from another hunter, older and supposedly more experienced than himself, the idea that you produced Gordon Setters simply by crossing English and Irish Setters.

Another tremendous uncertainty exists among the widest possible class of hunters

The Great Stylist of His Breed—the Irish Setter Dog, Smada Byrd's King

with reference to the so-called Llewellin Setters. Llewellin Setters are nothing more —and nothing less—than English Setters. Llewellin Setters are simply English Setters that trace back to two particular English Setters. They represent a certain definite English Setter ancestry. That's all there is to it. Thus an English Setter may not always be a "Llewellin"; but a "Llewellin" is always an English Setter.

Furthermore, the craze for this particular strain that came to this country with the importation of the first "Llewellins" caused ninety per cent of the owners of all Setters that are not either distinctly Irish or Gordon, to refer to their dogs as "Llewellins." Yet in ninety per cent of these cases, the dogs so referred to are not of the Llewellin strain at all. Not one person in a hundred who owns an English Setter can tell even from the pedigree whether the dog is of the Llewellin strain or not. They simply don't know. Most of those who refer to their Setters as "Llewellins" do so because the name is rather euphonious and pleasing to pronounce.

Many of those who really do know. insist

that their Llewellins be one hundred per cent, and they refer to those that are not as "grades." If there is even as little as three per cent "outcross," these few are inclined to feel that the dog is nothing but a rank plebeian. All of which is really ridiculous—at least so think a good many of us who have thought the matter out.

I am constantly getting letters that indicate a wide range of uncertainty in all these matters. I am always glad to get these letters—especially so since, as in the present instance, they enable me in writing to touch upon points that seem to have a common interest and in which there appears to be a somewhat common misunderstanding. Recently I received a letter from a man who asked for advice as to whether I would recommend his purchasing a Pointer or a Setter. He said he feared to get a Pointer because he understood they were hard to break. He hesitated to get a Setter because he feared the difficulty of burrs. Yet it is not much trouble to use scissors or clippers to remove the Setter's feathering, thus rather easily eliminating the annoyance of burrs when hunting in country where they abound. Furthermore, if the Setter is given plenty of work in the field previous to the opening of the season (which always *should* be done!) this very process of work will wear off the feathering to such an extent as to minimize the burr difficulty very materially.

But my correspondent was under the impression that Setters are easy to break and Pointers are hard to break! Just the reverse is true. There are, of course, exceptions. There are always exceptions to any rule. If you take fifty Setters, however, selected at random—and fifty Pointers selected equally at random—something way above the average number of the Setters will prove twice as hard to break as the Pointers. I am referring, of course, to those which have enough natural "go" in them to be really worth while. A dog that is nothing more than a plug, of either breed, may be easier to finish on game—but in most such cases you don't have anything after he is finished.

I am thinking of the type that really sift out into the scenery and go somewhere looking for birds. The kind that simply point birds they can't much help but stumble across in the course of pottering around are never a great deal of help. Furthermore, their work is never tinged with the same sort of satisfying fascination that comes from hunting with a dog that shows some *class*.

Let no reader imagine that my remarks are tinged with prejudice. I am simply stating the facts. When I say that Pointers will average much easier to break than Setters, I mean just that. I do not, however, want it to be interpreted that I prefer Pointers to Setters. I have owned both breeds—and I like them both. What I want is the right sort of *individual*—and I don't care whether it is a Pointer or a Setter. I have seen some Pointers that I prefer to most Setters I have seen; and I have seen just as many Setters that I prefer to most Pointers I have seen. If there ever was a fancier of Bird Dogs whose feelings are more naturally unprejudiced than mine to any particular breed, I wouldn't know where to find him.

I have gotten a number of letters recently asking whether Irish Setters make good dogs for hunting ringneck pheasants. Why of course they do—though some of them don't! Neither will all English Setters nor all Gordons nor all Pointers. But I personally can't consider that the breed, or the color, will prove the final answer to that. It's just a case of securing the right individual and coupling this individual to the proper training. I have seen individuals of all breeds that were no good on pheasants—many of them no good on any kind of game, for that matter.

There are, of course, certain breed characteristics of a general sort—yet even in the case of these there are always exceptions. It is pretty generally true, I think, that Gordon Setters are not so fast as the other breeds; and Irish Setters not so stylish. It is pretty generally true that the Pointer can hunt longer in a warmer climate without water; and that English Setters are pretty apt to hunt more merrily and attractively, having less tendency to pick the easy footing in their hunting. It is also true, I am positive, that each of the breeds can be improved by judicious breeding and judicious development of individuals. Of this I am certain—and to prove it let's take the record as shown by the

National Championship. That gives us something tangible and definite to gauge by, which is the reason for selecting it.

The National Championship was first run in 1896 and that was at a time when the Setters were supreme. It was before the Pointer breed had been developed to the point of competing successfully with the Setters. In those days they usually ran separate stakes for the two breeds. The winner of the Setter stake was often matched against the winner of the Pointer stake—the Setters almost invariably winning out. In those days, because it was not considered the Pointer could successfully compete with the Setter, the professional handlers trained themselves to understand Setter temperament and to develop it. The finishing of a Setter is a more delicate job than the finishing of a Pointer, but the handlers realized it would profit them to "wait for the Setters to come." Thus it was that from 1896 until 1909 no Pointer had ever won the National Championship. In that year, however, the Pointer dog, Manitoba Rap, captured the title. That was the be-

An Oklahoma Pointer Dog Showing Both Stanchness and Style

ginning of the turning of the tide—but no one really realized it then.

From 1909 until 1914, English Setters continued to uphold the belief of their supremacy. But in 1914, another Pointer dog captured the title, this being Comanche Frank.

About this time, the handlers began to pay more attention to the Pointer. He was easier to break. Therefore, if he could win over the Setter, he was a more profitable proposition from a monetary standpoint. It required less time to finish him—and he would begin to win earlier in life. The old Setter handlers began slowly one by one to pass out of the picture; and the younger generation of handlers came with strong Pointer sympathies. In spite of this, however, another English Setter proved supreme in 1915. This was the famous little bitch, LaBesita, "the last of the great Llewellins."

From 1915 until the present year, only two English Setters have ever won the National Championship at Grand Junction, Tennessee. The first of these was the dog, Joe Muncie, which won in 1918; and the second was

Feagin's Mohawk Pal, which won in 1926. In 1927 the title was again captured by a Pointer whose name was McTyre.

Now it so happens that Feagin's Mohawk Pal has been developed and is handled by a man who favors the Setters. Therefore, he lavishes upon his Setters undivided attention. He is in a position to do this because he hasn't even one Pointer in his kennels. He is exclusively a handler of Setters.

The point at issue is this, thus proving, I think, that we can succeed with what we concentrate on: Feagin's Mohawk Pal again won the National Championship in 1928. This gives him the title of National Champion twice out of five starts. He was Champion in 1926 and again in 1928. To win the title the second time, he competed against one of the largest entries in the history of the Stake; and he won *decisively*.

What is the lesson we can draw from this quick résumé of the National title? The answer is what makes it worth while to have discussed the subject. And the answer is, I think, a twofold one. First, judicious breeding can bring about a constantly nearer approach to perfection in the kind of canine we are striving to produce. The Pointer breeders have not had such finicky flights of fancy as seem to have beset the Setter breeders—with the result that the Pointer was developed until he could compete successfully with the Setters.

Secondly, we can see clearly, I think, that it is still possible for Setters to do their share of winning just as Feagin's Mohawk Pal has done in the National, provided the Setter is *handled understandingly*—a condition that is always so essential to results. A Pointer will stand rougher usage in training, while a Setter must be "gentled" into it.

CHAPTER VI

AVOIDING GUN-SHYNESS

THERE are certain phases of Bird Dog training that may be accomplished even during the breeding and summer seasons, and one of the most important of these is the *avoiding of gun-shyness.* I use the word "avoiding" advisedly—because an ounce of prevention is always worth a pound of cure—and there is absolutely no excuse for a gun-shy dog, if the proper precautions have been taken. Gun-shyness is always an evidence of—and a direct result of—poor handling. Since the avoiding of gun-shyness is so all-important in a gun dog, let us, therefore, devote this chapter to a discussion of this subject.

If one starts at the very beginning, a good way to get a young puppy accustomed to the gun is to fire one over him at feeding time. The plan perhaps works out best if there is a whole litter, or at least several, of the puppies together at the time. It can, however, be pursued with equal success with just one. The very young puppy, which has never had any reason to feel fear of man, nor any sort of intimidation, gives his first and foremost thought to food. Nothing else as yet has come into his life and the first law of nature takes natural expression. The test can be made by yourself—but more easily and surely if you have someone to help you. Let your helper take a *.22* caliber rifle and you carry the puppy's pan of food. First show the food to the puppy through the kennel wire and let him smell it so that his entire concentration is directed to the anticipated meal. While he is wigglingly eager to get at the contents of the pan, and as you go into the kennel with it for him, have your companion fire the rifle. There is almost no chance at all that the puppy will pay the slightest attention.

Before long you will be able to fire a shot from the rifle to give warning of your approach with the food, and the puppy will come to associate the gun with the feeding and consider it as a signal that feeding time has arrived. Thus his only thought of a gun, from the very earliest association, will be one of pleasure. You can soon change from the small rifle to a shotgun and preferably a 20-gauge—though even a 12-gauge should be perfectly satisfactory if a smaller one is not available and if the preliminary groundwork has been well laid. One secret of success in keeping the puppy fond of the gun is to *keep up* the shooting as a signal that it is mealtime. Don't do it just once in a while, or the proper effect will be lost. The gun must actually become to the pupil what the dinner bell is to the farm hand.

In the case of the "young hopeful" that has lived beyond the age of thinking more of his stomach than of anything else, a different plan than using the gun at mealtime should be used to accustom him to it, if his education with firearms has not been earlier begun. With a puppy from six months upward, that has never been introduced to a gun before, I prefer to start the acquaintance *in the field* instead of at mealtime. It is to be presumed —and it is important—that the puppy has already been given reason to have faith and *confidence in you.* The next thing is to introduce him to game and get him interested in it. In this case, it is important that his active enthusiasm in the hunting and finding of game should be aroused before the gun is brought into play. Forget the gun entirely until that has been accomplished. Then, if you have laid the groundwork well, there is but little chance that he will give the gun anything but a friendly thought when he first hears it.

It is always preferable, if at all possible, to start any introduction to the gun with as light a load as may be available. We are discussing, of course, the untried prospect. Our anticipation is to avoid any occurrence of gun-shyness. The cure of the disease is an entirely different matter. You must know that your puppy is not gun-shy—because you know that he has never had any occasion to be. You proceed, therefore, to find birds. Do not fire the gun until he has found them. It makes no difference whether he points or not—he may be, and I think should be, accustomed to the gun at an earlier age than that at which he may be stanch on his game.

So you go to the field and proceed to have a workout, the puppy reaching out to the birdy places and you carrying the gun. We suppose that he finds game—and flushes and chases it. That is the time for you to fire the gun in the air, while he is intent in trying to catch the fast flying birds. The unspoiled prospect will almost never fear a gun that is first fired under these circumstances. He will never fear it if his association with the weapon is carried along properly from this point forward. If it is in the open season, and you are close enough to kill a bird, so much the better. Killing is not essential, however, as the puppy's interest in the chase will be entirely sufficient to take his mind from any fear of the noise he hears; and if you keep up the same procedure a while, he will gradually come to consider the noise as a perfectly natural association with the pursuit of game.

The way gun-shyness develops in the first place is by taking a naturally timid dog and shooting over him too soon, or too much, or under the wrong conditions, or before you have first developed his friendship and love for you, and his confidence in you. It is no time to give a puppy his first introduction to a gun soon following chastisement. He must be up on his toes and keen and eager and confident and interested the first time he ever hears a gun. Food is a sufficient interest while he is still a wee one; and game is an equally sufficient interest at a later age.

Don't ever buy a puppy, or a grown dog either, and then start to test it for gun-shyness the first crack out of the box. That's the way gun-shyness is brought on. So many ignorant owners buy a dog, take him out of the crate and right into the field, while he is still strange to the new owner—and strange to his surroundings—and in a rather nervous state anyhow from a long railroad ride. The young dog that has never before heard a gun is pretty apt to become gun-shy in such circumstances; and many dogs that have never before been gun-shy, may be made so by such poor judgment. Gun-shyness is not necessary. Gun-shyness is always some man's fault.

I almost wonder whether to mention the cure of gun-shyness at all—because there will be no gun-shyness to cure if you follow the advice that has been given to avoid it. However, since we all know that gun-shyness does exist, perhaps we might as well mention one cure that the writer has tried personally and found successful. As a pretty general rule, it is about as cheap to buy a new dog as to try to cure gun-shyness. Different dogs may vary in their degree of merit in the field—but there is no weakness that makes a dog more worthless than gun-shyness. Different handlers have different methods of cure. Some of them sometimes succeed—but just as often they don't. It is also my personal belief that the *man* who is trying to effect the cure is just as important as the plan he may be using. The wrong man will fail with the right plan—where the right man might succeed even with the wrong plan. It is well to bear that in mind—as an evidence of how much depends upon *you.*

The cure in question was effected in the case of an English Setter bitch that came to me from Canada at two years of age and was found to be very gun-shy. The man who sold me this bitch didn't say anything about it—so I guess it was a secret. When I found out the existence of the disease, however, I gave up any and all thought of ever trying to shoot over this bitch again for some time to come. I spent the better part of a year just getting her to love me and to gain her confidence. During this time, I took her to the field as often as possible and worked her on birds. Never did we take a gun. I got the dog to love me and to have confidence in me, and to enjoy these trips afield.

When this had been going on for about a year—long enough, I felt, that the time had come either to prove a kill or a cure—I went out one day with some lightly loaded shells for my 20-gauge. I determined, however, not to shoot at anything under any circumstances except over a positive point. After a while, my English Setter found a covey. I flushed them for her, but this time did not shoot. The birds interested her to such an extent that she became busy immediately seeking the singles. Pretty soon she pointed one. I made up my mind this was the time for the test. As the bird was flushed, I shot and killed it. She was so intent and intense on her point that I doubt if she even heard the gun. She was thinking about something else much more important than a little noise. One after another we worked out those singles. I was careful as could be not to miss. I was shooting for high stakes and shot carefully and well. By the time we were through, I felt that her gun-shyness was a thing of the past.

But I wanted to be sure before saying too much, so we went again the following week. The same performance was repeated. No birds were shot at except over stanch points. Those that flushed wild flew away unharmed. I was playing a bigger game than merely to bag a few birds. When our second trip had drawn to an end, I knew beyond all question of a doubt that my splendid bitch was cured.

And so it proved. Since then, several other gentlemen have had the privilege of shooting over her, and she is no more gun-shy now than any of my other dogs. She is no more gun-shy than I am myself. In fact she simply loves a gun, almost more so than any dog I have ever seen. The reaction has been to the extreme. In view of my own success with this plan, I can recommend that it will work equally well for others if the steps leading to the ultimate test are carried out carefully. Therein lies the secret of success.

There are different degrees of gun-shyness. Some dogs are but slightly so. Some dogs don't especially like a gun, but are not just what might be called gun-shy. These cases will soon become worse, however, if the handling is of such a nature as to aggravate the condition rather than relieve it. It stands to reason, of course, that the degree the disease has reached is the matter that governs the difficulty of the cure. Some cases may be brought along simply, and almost easily. In other cases, only the most heroic efforts, amounting almost to genius, will bring about the desired results.

Speaking of gun-shyness, the worst kind of all is when the dog is not *always* afraid. With the dog that is always gun-shy, you have a much simpler problem than in the case of the dog that will some days stand for the gun in pretty good shape—and at other times flinch or actually fly for home. With this kind you *never know what to expect.* That makes correction all the more difficult. One day such a dog will work to perfection and not seem to mind the gun at all. He may even retrieve. He may even seem to take a keen pleasure in so doing. Then the very next time afield this same dog will bolt for home at the first crack of the gun—or at least sulk and quit hunting. You never have the same situation to contend with twice in succession. There indeed you do have a problem. It is quite possible, however, that much of this is brought about by a surly disposition, rather than being true gun-shyness.

The most fortunate thing about these rare cases is their rareness. The chances are that such a one as this may never come your way. But in case one does, my advice is that you exert double caution to get the dog's fullest confidence, in all that the term can imply. Be his companion and be his truest friend. Then, for a while at least, do not shoot over him for too long at a time. I have found this helps a lot. Even on days when he does not seem to mind the shooting—don't make a long hunt of it. Kill some five or six birds—or even less—and then quit. Quit while he is still keen. This unfinished hunt will linger and the chances are greater that the next time out the dog will take up where he left off before. He is not quite so apt to do this if you have shot over him to satiety the last time out. In other words, never shoot over him at any one time until he begins to tire, and his interest wane, at least not while there are any signs of the gun-shyness left in his system.

CHAPTER VII

RETRIEVING

WE HAVE discussed gun-shyness in the preceding chapter for the reason that the precautions to prevent this great fault belong really in the puppy age. Retrieving is something that may be taught at any time, hence perhaps this will be as good a time as any to discuss this phase of training.

There are many who do not even wish their Pointers or Setters to retrieve. In England it is not permitted—that is a job for Spaniels over there. Many fashionable hunters in this country are now following that practice and carrying along one or more Spaniels whose job is retrieving exclusively.

Retrieving is no longer required at our field trials. Judges do not score either for or against a dog that does it. There are several reasons. Stopping to retrieve slows up some dogs. They get to become potterers, nosing about for dead birds instead of resuming the hunt for new bevies. That is the reason some prefer two distinct types of dog—one to do the searching for game and pointing it, the other to seek dead birds after the kill.

There is another reason. It is next to impossible to keep the Pointer or Setter that retrieves *steady to shot and wing.* Some of them may remain steady if there is no kill—but let a bird fall and they're in to retrieve it before you can stop them. It is, of course, possible to prevent this—but not so unless you pay more attention to the dog than to the birds. And, in any event, your task is made doubly hard every time you hunt your steady dog with some friend's unsteady one—and we all know how often we find ourselves in such situations. Yet steadiness to shot and wing is not hard to maintain, even under trying circumstances, if our dogs do not retrieve.

Some of us, on the other hand, want our dogs to retrieve. We just naturally like to see them do it—we like their help "all the way"—and we don't like to run any chance of losing game. The last is most commendable.

Many dogs are natural retrievers. Nearly

all Spaniels are just "born to it." Some Bird Dogs take to it almost as naturally. With such as these all you need to do is cultivate the trait.

Always use the same command. Do not vary it—that but confuses. A dog's vocabulary of understanding is relatively small. Perhaps the one word "fetch"—is the best command to decide upon and stick to. In the hunting field I myself use three words: "Dead bird—fetch." Also, if I see my best retriever with a bird in her mouth at some distance from me, I say: "Bring it here." But my dogs are so constantly with me that they have a developed understanding. The shorter the command, and the fewer the words used, the better it will be as a rule. *And don't vary them.*

You may start at home with a rubber ball or old glove, if your dog shows a natural willingness to retrieve. Throw it for him and let him bring it back to you. But don't let him think it is just play—for some day he may not feel like playing and you'll be up against it. Therefore, even though he may show he likes it, make it a point always to

Perfect Retrieving

order him to "fetch." In that way he understands it as a command. It may be an order that he enjoys obeying—but it is an order just the same. This is very important if you would develop constancy in complying with your wishes. The transition is but slight from ball or glove to a bird in the hunting field, if you have laid the groundwork well.

There are dogs which will take rather naturally to retrieving a bird, but whose interest is not awakened by something so artificial as ball or glove. You kill a bird and the dog's first natural thought is to bring it to you. The minute you notice this tendency, and as the dog is doing it, say "fetch" gently and encouragingly. This encouragement is important so that the dog may not mistake the command at first for a rebuke. The tone of your voice will be his only way to understand that you are pleased.

Keep up the practice and you should soon have a good natural retriever. But practice makes perfect and the dog will improve with experience. Unless your dog just loves to retrieve—and even in that case I doubt if it is wise—never throw out a dead bird he has already brought you and ask him to retrieve it again. It helps, I believe, if every act you ask a dog to perform is backed by reason—and he knows there is no real reason for you to throw out birds already brought in, just to see him do the same thing twice. The serious and important aspect of the job suffers thereby in the dog's eyes—and that is sure to affect his work. I am, of course, speaking here of the natural, rather than the force broken retriever.

There is quite a question whether the force broken retriever will prove more dependable than one that is developed along "natural" lines. Many claim such is the case. Certainly in the case of the natural retriever you have no way to force the fulfillment of your desires if your dog suddenly takes it into his or her head that he doesn't care to do the job this time. In such circumstances a natural retriever can easily be ruined forever by wrongly applied abuse. In fact, *abuse* is never anything but wrongly applied. There is always a vast difference between abuse and punishment. The latter involves knowing what it is for.

Dogs that do not start to retrieve naturally must be force broken. It is well to perfect the pupil in the art of retrieving by a force system at some other period of the year than the actual shooting season. There are a number of different systems of force retrieving. The one which I shall outline has not only proven perfectly dependable, when followed correctly, but is also one of the simplest systems that the present writer has ever seen. Suppose you proceed carefully according to the following outline, step by step:

The best sort of an object to use in teaching retrieving is a corncob, for it is light, easily grasped, unoffensive to the taste and is easily replaced when soiled. A glove or pad absorbs saliva and is objectionable because of soon becoming soiled and offensive.

Adjust your training collar to the dog's neck, with the running free end on the upper side, and attach a short piece of stout cord thereto. Grasp this up close to the ring with the right hand and hold the corncob with the left hand in front of the dog's nose where he can easily see it. Give the command "fetch" in an ordinary tone of voice and accompany this command by a slight jerk or pressure on the collar. As the dog opens his mouth, instantly and gently place the cob in it, slackening the pressure of the collar at the same moment. Hold your left hand under his mouth and thus keep it closed on the cob. Soothe his fears and induce him to hold the cob steadily, caressing him if he holds it well. Do not hurry; but force him to take the cob again after a few moments. The first lesson should not be too long prolonged. Continue with this first lesson regularly, from day to day, until the dog will open his mouth promptly when you give the command to "fetch." Teach him to hold and carry the cob reliably without mouthing it. These lessons should be given in a well-ventilated room, avoiding any distractions, diversions or annoyances from spectators. A room has the further advantage of keeping the dog from cherishing ideas of escape, which may be his natural inclination during these early stages of training. In summer, the lessons should be given during the cool of early morning or late evening; and under no circumstances should they be continued until the dog is manifestly discouraged under the restraint of discipline. Never end a lesson abruptly or with punishment. Lead the dog about for a few moments, praise and reassure him, then take off the collar, thus concluding the lesson pleasantly.

Should the dog show great tendencies toward an uncontrollably hard mouth, this fault should be corrected at once. Prepare a device as follows: Through a piece of soft wood about the size of a corncob drive some wrought nails and clinch the ends around the outside of it. Put in enough so that he cannot grasp the wood without somewhere touching the nails with his teeth. After grasping it once harshly he may afterwards refuse to retrieve it. If so, force him to do it just as you began the lesson with the cob. All dogs have an intense dislike of closing their teeth on a hard substance. This device will enable you, after a bit of constant use, to effect tenderness in retrieving.

Having taught the dog to open his mouth promptly to the order of "fetch," the next stage is to teach him to step forward and grasp the cob. In this lesson you need several feet of stout cord attached to the training collar so that the dog is free to step forward when he hears the order. You hold the cob a few inches in front of the dog's mouth and on a level with it, where he may both readily see and grasp the object. Give the order to "fetch," exerting the necessary pressure on the collar at the same time and in a forward direction toward the cob, thus assisting him to grasp it. The moment the cob is in his mouth the collar must be instantly slackened. Be deliberate and praise the dog when he has done well. Continue such lessons in this manner until he will, without the pressure of the collar, step forward promptly and grasp the cob to the order of "fetch."

At this juncture of the early lessons the dog may continue holding the cob when you wish him to release it, being apprehensive that, if it is not in his mouth, the pressure of the force collar may follow. Reassure him kindly every time he surrenders it to command. If he will not let go promptly upon order, grasp the end of the cob in the left hand, but do not pull strongly on it. It is unwise to take it by *direct* force. When you have grasped the end of the cob with your left hand, command him to "give." Be prepared, if he refuses, to step on the toes of his forefoot. Use just enough pressure on his foot to force him to open his mouth—and this will require but little. After a few repetitions, he should surrender the cob instantly without punishment when the order to "give" is issued by you.

If you twirl the cob temptingly and playfully before the dog's nose, he may follow it in play and attempt to grasp it. It is a distinct gain if he will do so. Then he can be taught in a few lessons to pick up the cob. But too much playfulness should not be encouraged. The lessons should not lose the character of discipline. If too much playfulness is permitted, the force system will have no advantage over natural retrieving.

Having trained the dog so that he will step forward to grasp the cob as ordered, the next stage is to teach him to lower his head to grasp it. This is accomplished simply by the process of gradually lowering the cob, at first only two or three inches at a time so that the change of position is not too suddenly radical. If you can tempt the dog with the cob, by holding it in front of his nose, it should be easy to tempt him to follow it as it is lowered. If the dog takes kindly to this new lesson, he will sometimes even pick up the cob from the floor after a very few attempts, particularly if you are tactful and do not proceed in too much of a hurry. A dog which is really anxious to please requires very little punishment and there may not be any perceptible stages in his progress; in most instances the successive stages have to be formally and thoroughly observed. The dog requires time and schooling to comprehend his lessons. Hurrying him faster than he can comprehend or remember simply results in loss of time in the end.

At last the dog will pick up the cob when he is ordered to "fetch," provided it is held on the floor; but if the hand is removed, he may at first make mistakes. He has previously been guided by following the hand. He may still follow the hand—which results in confusion if the hand is not associated with the cob. By keeping the hand close to the cob, after the latter has been placed on the floor, the dog is induced to pick it up. Finally, after many repetitions, he should gradually disassociate the hand with the movements of the cob and learn to concentrate his attention upon the latter.

It must be admitted that it is sometimes difficult to persuade certain dogs to lower their heads. Some may be exceptionally obstinate in this respect. Force is the only answer in such cases. You must compel obedience. This means that you must be firm. It doesn't mean that you must be rough.

After the dog will pick up the cob, it may next be thrown a foot or two in front of him and give him the order to "fetch." In this lesson a longer check cord is required. If the dog doesn't move forward to the order, give him a jerk to start him forward and at the same time repeat the order. If the previous stages of the training have been hurried over too rapidly, or imperfectly taught, the effect will be more manifest now than at any previous stage. It may even be necessary to return to some prior stage of the development and begin all over again a progressive repetition. If the dog has been properly prepared up to this point, it should be easy. This lesson should be thoroughly and regularly given, until the dog is reliably trained to fetch the object promptly without the use of the collar.

Then he should be given practice on a dead bird. If he shows any tendency to be hard mouthed with this, you may tie some ten penny nails to the bird, which may be removed after he begins to pick it up and carry it tenderly.

When he will retrieve the dead bird well, which may require a number of special lessons, he may next be taken to the yard or even an open field for practice. Be sure that you have him under control—for if the pupil once learns that he may effect his escape from discipline by using his heels, you will but give yourself a new problem in control before the training in retrieving can proceed.

All dog training should be clear and free from confusion of any kind. Waters, in his book, relates a case in point. He tells of having observed a trainer who was earnest and industrious, but not wise. Waters says: "The cob was thrown out. The dog would start for it, and just before reaching it the trainer would give the sharp command 'Drop.' The dog was thus checked and confused; he did not know which order to obey. If he did not drop he was punished; and if he did drop he was then ordered to 'Fetch.' When he started to obey he was again ordered to 'Drop.' It is hardly necessary to add that the lessons were largely made up of violence and confusion. When the error of his method was pointed out to him, this trainer made rapid and easy progress teaching one thing thoroughly at a time."

No slovenly obedience should be accepted. Some men are satisfied if the dog brings the bird in and drops it close by. Do not accept such a performance, but insist that the dog complete his task. If you start slowly to walk away from him, this will often assist in inducing him to bring the bird in a direct line to you.

After your dog will "fetch" reliably, keep on continuing the lessons for many weeks so that the training will be indelibly imprinted upon his memory, and also to the end that perfect and prompt obedience may be established. He will then became so habituated to the work that disobedience or shirking never enters his mind.

In time, you may venture upon variations from the regular formality, with a view to developing the dog's intelligence. The cob may be shown to him and then thrown into bushes or tall grass, where he cannot see it, thereby forcing him to use his nose in finding it. The dog should learn to exercise a close watchfulness, this becoming an especially valuable trait later on in the case of marking down birds which fall to the gun in the hunting fields.

After you have done away with the cob, top off the training by using dead birds and perfect the dog in reliability in fetching and carrying. You may even school him to carry dead birds steadily to heel. You might drop a bird unobserved by the dog, but do it so that he will pass close and have a chance to smell it. Praise him highly if he picks it up. If he sniffs it but passes on, you should pretend to find it yourself and your manner should give evidence of pleasure at discovering such a prize, so that the dog's interest and desire to emulate may be aroused. Then require the dog to retrieve it. This program should be repeated from time to time until the dog will fetch a bird to a certainty when he runs across one accidentally. The result of this should be the bringing in of many dead or wounded birds of which the hunter may not have been aware.

As before mentioned, always insist on a perfect retrieve to hand. If you have adopted the method of giving him rewards, do not permit him to carry through his work or half do it, in his eagerness to get the reward. Insist on having every detail properly observed. Nothing is more annoying in practical work than the act of the dog in dropping a bird brought halfway in, or dropping the bird on the opposite side of a creek; or, when a wounded bird is dropped, necessitating a chase and retrieve on the part of the shooter, or another retrieve of the same bird on the part of the dog.

I was talking the other day with an old hunter who has some mighty good ideas pertaining to the art of practical retrieving in the field. This man sounds a warning against moving from your tracks when you send your dog in to retrieve. There is a lot of logic in it. His main point was that if you get to tramping and stamping around in the vicinity of where you think the bird should be, you confuse your scent with that of the game you seek—and simply make it that much harder for the dog. And that's true!

If a dog can smell a dead bird, he can also smell your scent—and where there are two scents, one is bound to have a diminishing effect upon the other. So there is mighty good logic in adopting the rule to stand perfectly still in one place and send your dog on to do the seeking for dead or wounded game. You will thus interfere with him less and he can do his job better.

There is another thing in favor of this. I have noticed in my own hunting that I have often confused a dog by attempting to aid him to find dead or wounded game. I could give a hundred instances—but will mention only one in particular. One day in Mississippi I marked down a bird that I was convinced I had killed outright. I was still at that time trying to help a dog retrieve—so I went to the spot I had marked as the location of the "dead" bird. My bitch could not locate and, between us, we tramped all about the place. Finally, the bitch was convinced the bird was not there and she began to circle out wider. I called her in—foolishly, as it turned out. I made her hunt close to where I was tramping about, although by then she was doing it unwillingly. Suddenly, my attention was attracted to a slight flapping of wings. The bitch crossed a tiny creek and to the point from whence came the sound, and *retrieved the bird I had supposed I had killed outright.* Yet it was still alive and the wing flapping had been done in its effort to crawl into a hole just a bit too small. Because of my procedure, I should have lost that bird entirely had it not been for the noise of its flapping. Yet—had I left the work entirely to the bitch, as I should have done—she herself would have retrieved that bird without my help, for I am sure she would have found it in the course of her circling after she had decided that the bird was not where we had both first supposed it to be. Many other such instances could be cited—but one such should prove enough.

There is another thing to commend the policy of the hunter standing still and letting the dog do the retrieving. If you want your dogs steady to shot and wing, you must be steady to shot and wing yourself. You are, of course, still steady to shot and wing if you do not break forward excitedly the minute you see a bird fall. However, if you do not go forward *at all,* how much stronger is the impression of steadiness made upon your canine companion!

There are, of course, exceptions to all rules. There will be occasions when an exception to this rule may be in order. But such exceptions only prove the rule.

There was, for example, the day in Mississippi when I dropped a bird that struck the ground running. When my bitch went to retrieve this bird, it ran and fluttered from her and she just missed its tail feathers as the bird dived in under an old abandoned cotton house. We surely had quite a time getting that bird! We could see it lodged in under the floor and made several attempts to reach it. Each time we got feathers, but the bird kept crowding in deeper and barely evaded us. We then went inside the old structure and pried up some of the loose floor boards with a pole. We thus finally caused the bird to flutter out into the adjacent field, where the dog followed and retrieved it.

But let's, as a rule, pledge ourselves to steadiness to shot and wing—and to *remain steady* while we send our dogs on to do the retrieving without so much attempted help as we are often inclined to try to give them.

CHAPTER VIII

BACKING

THE hunter who gets the truest and deepest enjoyment from a day afield with dog and gun is he to whom the little niceties have special appeal—the refinements, the *art* of the thing. And there is perhaps no refinement that deserves place beyond that of honoring the point of another dog, or "backing." Dogs that try to steal another's point—provided they do not actually flush the birds—may be shot over to some advantage; but there is a certain subtle something of satisfaction that is lost in the case of such a performance. The action indicates giving away to jealousy; and jealousy by either man or beast has no place in the hunting field. The little act of courtesy in honoring a bracemate's find is something that should be taught and encouraged —in fact, insisted upon—in all of our dogs.

From a purely practical standpoint, the dog so jealous that he refuses to back is always gambling with the hazard of flushing the birds. Thus backing is not merely a refinement—but has practical value as well. The wind may not be altogether right for the dog entitled to the find—but his nose may be keen—and the jealous competitor coming in from the wrong angle may easily spoil a shot. Be that as it may, it is the thrill produced by good dog work and manners that should give us the greatest joys from a day afield—and the satisfaction that surges through the hunter as one dog courteously honors the other is of a sort that should far exceed any that can come from the mere bagging of birds.

The present writer has observed that backing is more natural and easier to teach than pointing itself. This is particularly true of the young, high-strung individual—which is the kind most worth while, but also, by their very nature, the kind quite likely to develop jealousy later in life. Hence a word of caution may be injected here not to get careless later on and excuse your dog for failure to back. It is my belief that this often happens. In the early stages of development the puppy backs nicely; but the time may come when this very same puppy is keen to show out in front and his enthusiasm carries him to the point of forgetting his early training. That is the time when it is easy for an owner to get careless and feel that the thing may not happen again—that it was perhaps just an accident in this case. But the dog has more likely than not done it deliberately—and from getting by with apparent impunity, he forgets his early lessons and continues to take liberties until a serious situation develops. Such a case is harder to cure at that stage than it is to correct in the very beginning and hence constitutes something that it is well to guard against.

There is some division of opinion as to whether it is advisable to give a young prospect his first lessons in the field in company with an older dog, or alone. There is something to be said on both sides. Much can be accomplished by the experience of the older dog in finding the game to work on. And he sets the pupil a proper example to follow. On the other hand, there is sometimes a danger that the young hopeful may thus gradually lose his initiative and come to depend too much upon his more experienced bracemate to find all the game. From the stand-point of teaching a dog to back, however, this can be most easily taught in the early stages by having a tried and true bracemate along.

The younger dog, because of lesser experience, is not so apt to find the birds as is his older bracemate. Furthermore, when these finds are made, it is almost as natural for the young dog to back at sight as it is for him to chew a bone. He is still in the formative stage. His jealousies are not aroused. As is natural for youth, he looks up to and respects his elders. The attitude of the dog on point attracts his attention and it is the most natural thing in the world for the young dog to imitate his superior in that action. Boys like to imitate men; and puppies like to imitate grown dogs. So the art of backing becomes an easy thing to teach—in fact, you scarcely have to teach it.

It is important, however, that you be alert to the time when this same puppy, which backs so beautifully now, gets into the high school or college age of feeling his own oats. Then he begins to have a mind of his own. Then he likes to show off and do as he pleases.

Then he is almost a grown dog—and thinks he's as big as any man's dog. By that time he has learned something of finding game on his own responsibility—and has made some points of his own. Then is when he may no longer be content to take a back seat and honor another dog's work. He is then at an age when he wants to jump over the traces and do things on his own responsibility and in his own way. Watch out for that day—and be careful that you keep him in line, and permit him no undue liberties.

It is a mighty good idea to take great pains always to show approval to a dog for backing. It will help you if you pay even more attention to the backing dog than you do to the dog that is pointing. Go first to the backing dog and stroke him gently, speaking quiet words of encouragement. Make him feel that he is doing the right thing. Make him glad that he is—and show him that you are glad. That will make him feel like he's the fellow in the limelight and he will come to consider that he is more to be envied for backing even than is his bracemate which has the find. Those who are careless in this particular will have more trouble with their dogs failing to back than will he who is particular about this important evidence of appreciation.

Thus we find that there is little or no difficulty at all connected with teaching backing to a dog that begins his field training in company with a bracemate. The important thing is simply to see to it that your dog always keeps on doing what he has been taught to know that he should do. If you have always been alert to show as much appreciation of a back as you have of a point, you won't have much trouble. If you have not taken that precaution, or if you have been careless about making sure that your dog always backs properly, you may soon see evidences that give you cause for concern.

Some dogs are taught to point on their own responsibility before they have ever seen any other dog "get there first." There are exceptions to all rules, but the chances are that a dog so trained will not back so easily nor so naturally as the kind we have been talking about. Many prefer to teach pointing first, however, and there is much to commend it. A dog learns to find birds on his own responsibility and thus is not always playing second fiddle in his most important development period. If he doesn't try to steal the point the first time he is ever beaten to the birds, all will be well and precaution on your part is all that is necessary. In this case, when your young dog first backs, you want to get to him and lay your hands on him gently, uttering words of encouragement. Show him as much evidence of appreciation for backing as you have ever shown when he has been pointing. That very thing may help you to win the battle right there. Keep him steady on his back as long as possible. Let the point be held by the dog having it while you are working with your prospect. Don't let it be just a temporary pause. Impetuosity in the hunting field is never to be encouraged anyhow either by man or beast. It won't hurt either dog to maintain his attitude long enough to let your pupil get it through his head that he deserves as much praise when he honors as he does when he points.

If the pupil is already steady to shot and wing, and if you are alone, you may shortly go forward and flush the birds. But it is

Two Setters Handling Ring-neck Pheasants. Snappy Dogs *CAN* Handle Them

usually well to have a companion with you to do the flushing, while you devote your attention to keeping the backing pupil steady to wing. A few repetitions of the performance should soon accomplish the desired result of dependable backing. If, however, he commits an error, he should be taken back to where it was committed and made to accept the correction there. And for yourself, always remember never to rush forward the minute birds are flushed. More dogs are made unsteady to shot and wing by undue excitement on the part of the handler than most of us imagine.

If your pupil does not back naturally at sight, the only thing to do is use a check cord and bring him up to the proper distance behind the other dog on lead with the instrument available to make sure that he does what you want him to do. The procedure is exactly the same, except that in the one case you have means of control in the form of the check cord (either with or without a choke collar); and in the other case you don't. It often happens that dogs which have once backed, later develop jealous dispositions that cause them to cease doing so; and a great many of these may require a little work with the check cord, perhaps reënforced by a choke collar, in order to make them behave and resume their perfect performances.

The late C. B. Whitford once told me that none of us would have quite so much trouble with backing if we weren't so infernally afraid our dogs weren't going to back. He said a dog was once brought to him for correction and, even before he saw him perform, he made a wager with the owner that the dog would back if no commands were shouted at him to make him do so. Mr. Whitford's agreement was that he would pay the wager, if the dog failed to back, provided the owner would positively not forget himself and remain absolutely mute. His theory was that cautioning a dog, before giving him a chance to back on his own volition, simply excited him unduly and actually encouraged creeping in.

Whitford claimed that he won the wager. It should be well understood, however, that his idea in connection with silence merely involved giving the dog a *chance* to do right before cautioning him. In other words, it is a mistake to go on the assumption that he is going to do wrong and start cautioning him before he has done it. From that angle, I believe there is a lot in his theory.

On the other hand, however, in the case of the dog that has come to a backing attitude, and then begins to sneak in, it is manifestly careless for the handler to stand by and not speak a word of restraint. In this case, if a dog has been yard broken and taught the meaning of the word "whoa," this command should be used to steady him, whether he be pointing independently or backing another. But don't ever shout a command. Speak as softly as possible though as firmly as necessary. You will get far better results. Easy firmness quiets a dog and encourages obedience. Shouts of command only excite the animal. Excitement only leads to confusion. A quiet confidence is the aim to strive for.

If a dog doesn't mind you, don't run at him. Where mental poise is so needed, the worst thing you can ever do is to upset that poise. If a dog fails to mind, see to it that he does. Even if he sneaks in on his bracemate to the unfortunate extent of flushing the birds, you only make matters worse if you shout and rush to get to him. If he fails to heed a firmly spoken command, he is surely going to be heedless of an excited command shouted at him. Stand where the error was committed and make him come back to you. He will do it if you haven't excited him. Then correct him. Make him stand where he was and where he should have stayed. Hold him there. Begin gradually to show approval of him for staying there. Increase your encouragement, but do not pamper him. Physical punishment will not be necessary—and is more likely to have only a harmful effect—unless it is in the case of the fully finished dog old enough to know that he has deliberately done wrong. The dog that knows he has done wrong expects to be punished and should be. Every possible allowance must be made, however, before administering punishment.

And if you are going to punish a dog, don't call him to you for that punishment. You go to him. That's the only fair thing to do. Then take him back to where the error was committed and administer the punishment there. Some men may be sure enough of their dogs to dare to command them to come in for their punishment, even knowing what they are to expect. But you're really not playing square with him by making him come in for his own medicine. You go to him.

CHAPTER IX

TEACHING TO POINT

THE proper age at which to begin seriously to develop the art of pointing may vary. Much depends upon the characteristics of the individual dog. Another factor is whether you plan to use the pupil exclusively as a shooting companion—or whether you have field trial aspirations. In the latter case, the pressure of restraint should be longer delayed, while the prospect is cultivating his "natural" qualifications—a certain freedom of speed and range, experience in using his nose, and a knowledge of the habits of game birds.

The younger the pupil at the time you ask him to quit his flushing and chasing, the greater the chance of "cramping his style." Dependable pointing, without independent search, is but little to be desired. Let it be ever remembered that you can almost always stop a dog up. But you cannot always get a dog to go out. Even if your dog is to be but your shooting companion, and hence need not have quite field trial range, you still should want him to show keen searching initiative. Therefore, do not cramp this by trying to get him to "handle" his birds dependably at too tender an age. It is far better to take your time and "wait for him to come down to it." You must have patience, and use rare good judgment in your proceedings, if you want to end up with a *hunting* dog—and not just one that merely points. *Finding* is ever more important than pointing—and if this were not true Spaniels would have but little value as gun dogs.

Puppies five or six months old may be taken afield and shot over. But never work such young ones very long at a time. A couple hours—at the most—is enough. Too much, if the puppies show signs of beginning to tire.

Some puppies at six months may start to point naturally. All well and good. But six months is fully a year too early to bear down heavily on the keen kind. You'll *take too much out of them,* if you do. Furthermore, you want a dog to go to his birds *positively* and with *decision.* Early pressure tends to make creeping potterers and false pointers. So don't bear down too much too soon—or you may bring on all sorts of faults. Among these may be mentioned over-cautiousness, false pointing, indecision, and on occasion, such even greater crimes as blinking or bolting. *So take it easy!*

Whether your pupil be Pointer or Setter, the work of teaching to point may best be accomplished if based upon a classification of individuals—not a breed classification, but a classification according to the characteristics of the dog himself. Under this system of classification, there will be no distinctions between Setters and Pointers.

Offhand, we believe, your dog will fall in one or more of the following eight classifications: (1) Slow and close; (2) Fast but close; (3) Wide—whether fast or slow; (4) Natural pointing instinct; (5) Natural tendency to chase; (6) Keen and courageous; (7) Phlegmatic; and (8) Keen but timid.

The procedure in developing the art of pointing will perhaps find its best results if the method is adapted to the pupil. The proper procedure in the case of a dog of certain characteristics may be exactly the wrong method in the case of opposite characteristics.

Although we have classified eight different general types, we well realize that many dogs may combine two, or even more, of the classifications. For example, two different dogs may each be wide; but one may be wide and slow, while the other is wide and fast. In like manner, a dog very keen to hunt may have a highly developed natural pointing instinct; while a phlegmatic hunter may have a very hard-headed instinct to flush and chase.

Be all that as it may, the classifications as given will suffice for the purpose at hand; and will, we think, serve best our purpose of trying to differentiate between types in order that the art of pointing may be taught with the least lost motion and with the hope of leading to the final result by the most direct route.

According to the older systems of dog training, still in vogue in England, and also in this country to a certain extent, the handler has perfected his pupil in a course of yard breaking before ever taking the dog into a field that may contain game. While the writer is not a confirmed and fast believer in the necessity of previous yard breaking, he nevertheless recognizes its merit, particularly for certain types. Such yard breaking may become almost essential in the case of a very keen dog which lacks natural pointing instinct and is a wide worker. Such a dog is apt to be so far away from you when he finds and chases birds that some method of control becomes vitally essential. If you feel that your prospect is one of this kind, you had better proceed with a course of yard breaking at once.

Such a course should include to *whoa* at command or signal. For close workers, the spoken word may suffice. Wide dogs will require some signal given by a motion of the arm. Take a pan of tempting food, a check cord, and your dog, to a spot where you will be alone. Place the food at some little distance from the dog, but let him see it and know where it is. Attach the long check cord to his collar (a choke collar, if necessary) and then let him start for the food. Just before he gets to it, stop him with the check cord and speak the word "whoa" firmly at the same instant. Don't be rough. It can't possibly accomplish any good and may easily accomplish much harm. Be kindly firm. That's all that is ever necessary. Don't tire the dog or annoy him by a too prolonged repetition of the thing. You may and should, however, repeat the procedure three or four times at each lesson. Make him stand steady for several minutes each time. Speak the word "whoa" to him quietly at frequent intervals. Put your hands on him and make him stand as though posing at a bench show, repeating quietly and encouragingly the word "whoa." When this has been repeated three or four times, stopping him artificially on each occasion just before he reaches the food, you may finally give him the food as his legitimate reward—and then close the lessons for the day. Continue these lessons daily until you have so perfected the pupil that you may have confidence you could stop him with the word "whoa" when he winds birds in the field, just as successfully as you are able to stop him with the command when he is approaching food. The battle of breaking is half won if you proceed along this line.

In much the same manner that you teach the dog to whoa, you can teach him to down charge—stay in one place—or do anything else that you may wish to order him to do. Let us repeat a word of caution here—always use the same command for the same order. Never switch words and thus confuse the dog. If you wish him to stop and stand, the commonly accepted word "whoa" is as good as any—or you may select any other that you prefer just so long as you never vary it. If you wish to teach the dog to drop, you may use that word, which is easy and short; or you may use the word "down," or the word "charge." Select one of these and stick to it. You stop the dog just as you do in the case of teaching him simply to whoa; but when you go to him you give a new command—"down"—and gently press him down to the ground at the same time. Repetition of this will perfect him in the art of dropping at command just as promptly as he obeys the command to "whoa." From these steps you may proceed to the use of signals. A good

Pointing Quail in Virginia—the Field Trial Winning Setter, Buzz Detour

signal for the whoa command is to hold your arm aloft, palm outward; and a good signal when you wish the dog to drop is simply to lower your arm emphatically. It is scarcely necessary to add that such signals are serviceable only when you know that your dog sees you.

If the dog is not in sight when you wish to give a signal, it is necessary to whistle him in. A good loud whistle is essential for a dog handler, whether he be amateur or professional, and there are a number of very satisfactory different kinds on the market. The present writer has a personal preference for a large wooden whistle, due to the fact that this can be put to the lips at any time of year with perfect impunity. On a very cold day, a metal whistle may scalp all the skin off your lips. On the other hand, the best metal whistles will perhaps reach your dog at a greater distance and are perfectly satisfactory in every way unless suddenly placed to the mouth in zero temperature. In the South this objection is never so vital. It may also be overcome in any temperature by warming the whistle in the hand before using it.

A good many trainers at the present time introduce their dogs to game without giving them any previous course of instruction such as above outlined. In the case of dogs falling under several of the eight classifications, this plan has quite a little to commend it. The most uninteresting canine companion in the world is the dog that is overly mechanical. He may never make any mistakes; but, by the same token, never will he rise to the occasion with a sparkling performance that demands independence of action and genius of execution. Yard breaking may take a certain amount of initiative away from some dogs and lean them toward the mechanical kind of performance. A dog can't figure out why in the world you want him to whoa a few feet from a pan of food. He may be taught to obey this command—but its reason still remains a mystery. The same thing performed in the field, in the presence of game, has a different aspect. That's the *real thing!* Furthermore, the handler is aided by generations of inherited pointing instinct—which aid is entirely lacking in the artificiality of a course of yard breaking.

For the above reasons, dogs that fall under several of the eight classifications we have listed may be given their first lessons in the field without having been yard broken first. Those classifications surest to fall within the scope of this possibility would be: the close rangers; those with a lot of natural pointing instinct; and the phlegmatic ones. Even dogs that might fall under the classifications of bold, keen hunters, might be so handled provided they would also qualify under the classification of a highly developed natural pointing instinct. The same is equally true of the wide ones with a highly developed pointing instinct—though the keener they are and the wider they are and the faster they are, the less likely you are to control them satisfactorily without previous yard breaking. Yard breaking will save a world of work and worry if your dog has a combination of the following qualities: fast, wide, keen hunter, whose natural instinct is more toward chasing than pointing. Just the same, this is the very kind that—when once controlled—will usually make the finest dogs of all.

If you are working your dog in the field

and he establishes a point which he will hold long enough for you to get to him, the battle should be almost won then and there. Do not rush at the dog, but go to him quietly and quickly so that you may get your hands on his as soon as possible. That is your great chance to steady him. You might raise his tail, if he holds it too low. If his attitude is not high headed, gently lift his head into a patrician attitude. In short, work with him long enough that he will understand that pointing is not simply a temporary pause—but a permanent attitude *to be held as long as the birds are there.*

While working with the dog in this position, it is a rather good idea to use a little easy pressure from behind, gently pushing him toward the birds. His natural tendency will be to back up against this pressure, to keep from flushing. Even dogs that might go in and flush of their own volition, will resist such likelihood of a flush from an artificial source. A few repetitions of this kind will soon bring about complete steadiness to point. The greatest of all secrets, in making a dog point truly and hold, lies in getting your hands on him so as to be able to make manifest that he is expected to point with dependable steadiness.

With one of the wide ones, of the kind that require an artificial stimulation of the pointing instinct, it is a good idea to take the dog into birdy territory, with an old reliable bracemate, and keep the pupil on lead while the other dog finds birds. When game has thus been located, you can lead the young dog up until he winds the birds himself—and then proceed the same as above outlined. It is sometimes a good plan to pick up the pupil when you see the other dog point, and carry him to the proper position. There is something about this, when he suddenly gets the scent of game, that will tend to stiffen and steady him up on his own account. Keep up this work until you have reason to believe the dog may perform properly of his own accord—then try the pupil out alone. The more inclined your dog is to chase, the longer will you have to continue the use of a bracemate and the plan of artificial control. You will have to be the judge of when it is proper to make the first attempt to let the dog handle his own birds.

Some trainers like to work a dog with a long dragging lead trailing out behind. This is all right in some cases. With a dog that hunts too close anyhow, this restriction is not necessary and should not be used. Too much cramping of range is always to be discouraged, unless you desire an especially close ranging dog for some kinds of cover. In most cases, where the plan is properly used, the trainer hopes that the dog will at least pause on point long enough so that he can get to the end of the lead and put his foot on it before the dog flushes. If this can be accomplished, you hold the dog in position as you work up to him hand over hand—then proceed the same as previously outlined to handle him and steady him until he understands what it is all about and what you expect him to do.

If you are working your pupil without a lead, should he find and flush birds, you must immediately mark the spot where the flush occurs, by dropping your coat or hat there, and then bring the dog back to this spot as soon as you can do so and there pose him in pointing position and hold him for some little time, steadying him by both hand and voice—thus letting him know that he should have stood as you are now showing him how to do, and that his chasing was an error. Mere pointing is one thing—but dependable steadiness, so that you may know your dog will *be there,* with his birds, no matter how long it takes you to find him, requires great patience on your part. Do not expect results in a minute—or even a week or a month!

Dogs so keen or so wide or so fast that they cannot be perfected in pointing by the various means as outlined are rather more than the average amateur should tackle with hope of success; but the ordinary amateur, with the average dog, should accomplish results by pursuing one or several of the plans as outlined. The services of a reliable professional handler may be required for dogs that do not respond to this treatment.

CHAPTER X

STEADINESS TO WING AND SHOT

ONE of the real refinements in the art of handling game is steadiness to shot and wing. Dependability on point is essential. Without that, a hunt may be spoiled. Steadiness to shot and wing is not exactly essential from the standpoint of merely bagging birds. Perhaps that is one reason it is so often neglected when one is afield and his dogs break shot in the excitement of a hunt.

Steadiness to shot and wing is *easier to teach than to maintain.* There are a number of reasons for this. Such steadiness is something that is not, and cannot be, taught until dependability on point has been accomplished. Reliability on point is in itself a contributing factor toward making steadiness to shot and wing the next step in the process. The means by which "breaking shot" is cured will be found to accomplish the desired result with gratifying positiveness.

The inclination of most dogs, when birds

are flushed, is to go with them. Only a few dogs are naturally steady to shot and wing. Most of them break at the flush and seem to think that, if they go fast and far enough, they can be there when the birds 'light again. This of itself is a helpful contributing factor in the long run, for an intelligent dog will finally learn that it simply can't be done. For this reason, a dog should be permitted to go ahead and do his chasing at the flush until you are ready to steady him down, and surely until you have accomplished a positive dependability on point. Then you may take up the refinement, after your dog can be trusted to hold his birds on point.

The correction method is simple and so positive that but a very few applications should be required. You carry your long training lead, which should be a stout one for this purpose, and let your dog find game, which he points steadily. You go to him and snap the training lead to his collar while he is on point. You wrap the other end of it a couple of turns around the hand so that you *know* you have it firmly in your grip. Then you are prepared to step up and flush the birds just as you have been doing. One person can do it, though two can work to better advantage. If you have a companion, let him do the flushing while you handle the dog.

As the birds take wing, the dog goes with them just as he has been doing. You want to brace yourself now! Just before he reaches the end of the forty foot training lead, call "whoa" to him very firmly. He won't pay any attention—but you want to start the use of the signal which he is to associate with what will follow the next instant. About the time you get the word "whoa" out of your mouth, the dog will have reached the end of the check cord. If he is going fast enough, and you have set yourself to resist the impact, when he reaches the end of the line he is going to be treated to about the most complete somersault he will ever know in a long career. One such somersault will usually deplete his desire to depart with the birds.

If one such severe lesson is not enough, two should surely do it; and if two are not enough, you may try it with a *choke collar*. If that doesn't cure him, I'll give up! Any dog that will continue to chase when he knows that every chase means a tumble will be a rare creature indeed.

There may be, of course, certain cases where you might have difficulty. The trouble the writer had once was that the dog went away with such vim, and I was so surely set for him, that the rawhide training lead snapped as if it had been hit with an ax. But only a few dogs will hit one that hard—and that lead was an old one anyhow. Furthermore, I wasn't using a choke collar—in fact, I never have.

Another case when I had difficulty was with a dog that, while he chased at flush, never put enough real dash into it to get a jarring spill. He never hit the end of the lead hard enough to be turned over. Consequently, what should have been a severe lesson was so tame that it amounted to almost nothing. With the phlegmatic type of dog—one that will not hit the end hard enough to get a jolt—the only thing to do is to snap on the check cord and simply *hold the dog* steady when you flush the birds, so that he cannot go away with them, speaking the word "whoa" as you hold him steady. In other words, by simply holding him steady to flush, he gradually learns that such steadiness is demanded. This method is apt to take a little longer because it is not severe enough to drive the thing home with one big dose.

Even when you have steadied your dog to shot and wing, it is a good safety measure to keep on going to him and snapping the lead to his collar. Do this at least for a while. The value of this is that he knows the thing which can turn him over is there; and that's what you want—to let him think that you have the power at command to control him. Even after he becomes so steady that you feel fairly sure of him, it isn't a bad idea to take just a little precaution by going to him on point and take hold of his collar as though you were in the act of snapping on the lead. It's a good plan to make him *think* it's there, even after it really isn't. Don't take too much for granted. Don't get careless. It is better to be safe than sorry. And if you admire a finished performance, a little effort is well worth while.

As previously stated, there isn't any phase of training where corrective measures with more positive results are possible. Before a dog points and holds long enough for you to get to him, there is mighty little you can do. You are almost helpless until you can get your hands on him. But that isn't the case at all in teaching steadiness to shot and wing —for you don't even start until steadiness on point has been accomplished. Many may wonder, then, why so many dogs break shot.

Some trainers prefer to make their dogs *drop* to shot or flush. This is taught by going to the dog on point and ordering him to "drop" before you flush the birds—and pressing him down to the ground if need be. If you make him *stay* down, he can't get away so easily and a dog already perfected in obedience can be handled to advantage. The thing in favor of this plan is that a dog, in a crouching attitude, by the very nature of his position, is not so prepared to dash away with the birds, and hence is not so inclined to do so. Most any dog realizes that, if he can't break the instant the birds break, he has a hopeless task ahead of him. When he sees that the birds are gone, he realizes the hopelessness of trying to catch them and this favors the plan of teaching your dog to "drop" before you flush or shoot.

On the other hand, a dog crouching in heavy cover cannot mark the birds down; and it is often a great aid to the hunter in following the singles, if the dog, as well as himself, has some idea where they have gone. However, it is better to have a dog drop to shot than to break shot. It is also a pretty performance—there is something so submissive about it that it has almost as much appeal as perfect steadiness in an upright position. But even with all that dropping has to commend it, it cannot quite be classed with the erect performance where a perfectly dependable dog stands steady and marks with his master the flight of the birds.

Steadiness to shot and wing denotes the fully finished performance. Why then, since it is not difficult to teach, do we see so few which fulfill such finish? The answer brings up a number of things. In the first place, so many dogs are not steady to shot and wing that owners wonder if it is worth while to perfect their own. The chances are that the fellow you shoot with has a dog that is not steady. Thus you may wonder what is the use in trying to make your own steady. If the majority of Bird Dogs were steady to shot and wing, the fellows owning the unsteady ones would be more ashamed of them than is the case to-day—and the result would be that we would see more steady dogs than we do now except in the field trials, where steadiness is demanded in All-Age stakes.

In England, they concentrate more on perfection of manners than we do here in America. One reason for this is that *they have more game* over there and hence more opportunities to develop a finished dog. Another thing is that they have so much game they do not need to be continuously thinking about the next find—but may concentrate more on the proper handling of each in turn. All foreign handlers take great pride in the perfection of manners they teach their dogs when on game. But all foreign countries are older than ours and hence most of them have found out from experience what we have yet to learn—that active and intensive game *propagation* is just as important as game protection, perhaps even more so. The result is that they really have game to protect over there—so much, in fact, that the job of adding polish to a Bird Dog's manners is simplified. In our younger, more impetuous country, we lack the sort of patience that leads to such perfection of manners as they insist upon abroad.

Reverting back to the subject before us, we hope we have shown that steadiness to shot and wing is one of the least difficult things to teach in the repertoire of Bird Dog training. Once learned, we should have little further difficulty—provided we might always hunt our dog alone. But the fact is that we can't or don't do this. You know how you will get involved on hunts with other fellows who want to work their dogs with yours; and that's when the trouble creeps in. The chances are such dogs will be unsteady and this is almost sure to work toward either a prompt or gradual return of unsteadiness in your own, unless you are mighty careful. In such cases, we are too apt to think: "Oh, well, that won't happen again;" and hence we are likely to let the digression go without correction. That is bad. We only make it harder for ourselves and harder for the dog.

If you let him keep bad company, the influence can easily become lasting—more easily in a mature dog, in fact, than in the case of a young one that is not yet even supposed to be fully finished. If you get in with friends who have unsteady dogs, the fairest thing for your own is to separate and hunt him alone in a different direction. Any man has a right to be particular about his dog and his gun. He *should* be.

There is another situation that can bring about what might be classified as unsteadiness, though that to which we refer is not in our judgment of a very serious nature, and certainly not to be classified with the fault of unsteadiness that comes about simply from a desire to chase. We have in mind *breaking shot to retrieve.* I really don't like to call this breaking shot—rather do I prefer to call it going in a bit quickly to recover game that falls to the gun.

Many dogs that will not budge from their tracks at flush or shot, if game doesn't fall to the gun, will go forward before ordered on when they see birds drop. But it is *possible* so to perfect your dog in steadiness that he will not move even when game is killed, until ordered on to retrieve. This is but an added step to the steadiness as first taught. It certainly shows beautiful manners if your dog resists the temptation to recover dead birds until he is told to do so.

On the other hand, dogs are intelligent creatures and practical experience in the field is pretty apt to show your canine companion, in the course of time, that some game which falls to the gun may not be recovered if prompt retrieving is overlooked. Wing-tipped birds may run and get away. Such birds may be lost if the dog is held back too long. An intelligent dog reasons this out and the time may come when he begins to take matters into his own hands and goes forward without waiting for your order. Certainly it is true that this may be the means of saving a lot of game. From that standpoint, it is justifiable and excusable, always provided the dog is going in solely for the purpose of retrieving and not with any thought of chasing the flushed birds. The latter is never excusable and has nothing ever to justify it.

The chief objection to the dog going in too

Steady to Wing and Shot—the Pointer Dog, Hotentot, a Sensational Field Trial Winner

quickly to retrieve comes in the case of being hunted with a bracemate. Such performance when hunting alone has very little, if anything, to be said against it. But, if you are hunting with some friend whose dog is steady even to the kill, he may object to the influence of your dog on his own if yours goes in ahead of orders. Or, you may be hunting your dog with another that doesn't retrieve at all (many don't). In this case the other dog doesn't associate the action with the thought of recovering game—but the effect on him is the same as breaking for the purpose of chasing. Thus if this dog which doesn't retrieve is steady to shot and wing, a harmful influence has been placed in his path.

The present writer has a dog which is steady as a rock to shot—and *was* steady even if a bird was killed. One day, however, I wing-tipped a pheasant in an open field and the bird lit running. That was too much for the little Setter and she broke to get him, which she did. How was I to punish her for that? She knew the bird would have gotten away if she hadn't done just that thing—and I knew it—and she knew that I knew it. She knew that we were there to get that bird. What answer could I give her had I punished her for something which accomplished the exact result for which we were afield?

But there has been an aftermath. I have another dog that doesn't retrieve. The little bitch now goes in the minute a bird drops and promptly brings it back to me. The result is that we lose mighty little game. But my non-retriever doesn't quite understand it. He can't figure why he isn't permitted to "break" with his bracemate. Perhaps the fault is all my own in not having made retrievers of both of them. But even if that were the case, *two* dogs rushing forward present a very different situation from one going in too quickly. Two of them are sure to lead merely to confusion; and confusion has no place in any hunt. Jealousy would also soon develop—and that is equally bad.

It will thus be seen that, while steadiness to shot and wing is much to be desired, and is not difficult to teach in the first place, there are many complications which militate against continual perfection unless diligent care is used. If we insist on maintaining perfection on the theory of perfect manners, we are apt to do so at the cost of a certain amount of game; and if we permit a slight breach in the rules in order to accomplish the practical, we are almost sure to lose something somewhere else. So it might seem as broad as it is long. Breaking shot is unquestionably one of the unsolved problems in the case of most gun dogs to-day.

Perhaps the complications make one of the real reasons why so many American Bird Dogs are not steady to shot and wing. We are torn between two fires. The result is that we don't put out either of them. I must be frank enough to confess that it is really a problem. We will conclude the discussion by straddling the issue—and excusing what may be classified as merely too much promptness in retrieving; but, in the very same breath, we definitely deplore unsteadiness of any other kind—or for any other reason. There is no excuse for permitting a dog to break shot except for the one purpose of retrieving—and this can scarcely be classified as breaking shot in the true sense of the word.

CHAPTER XI

BOLTERS

YEARS ago bolting dogs were almost unknown. They are a product of our field trial system of developing speed and range. Today bolters are sufficiently prevalent to warrant a chapter devoted to their discussion. It is true, of course, that bolters seldom or never appear among dogs developed strictly along shooting dog lines; yet now and then an average hunter will get hold of a dog with bolting tendencies and the questions that have come to me indicate that these present a problem that many owners do not understand. It seems logical, therefore, to devote these few pages to a discussion of bolters, which will naturally lead us also into the subject of speed and range, on which there is such a wide variance of both opinion and conception.

The reason we had no bolters of old was because little or no thought was ever given to an artificial development of more speed or more range. Game was plentiful and not hard to find. Thus all effort was concentrated upon the proper *handling* of game. But little attention was paid to the matter of *finding* game, except as different dogs varied naturally in their ability to do so. Some were, of course, much better than others; but this ability was attributed to natural nose, natural range, natural speed, natural birdiness. The good dogs were praised then as now; and the poor ones condemned; but that is about all there was to it.

Then, in 1874, the first field trial was held near Memphis and thus public competition between Bird Dogs was given birth. At first, the judging was based on the old point system of scoring. Later, we came to the heat system; and later still, to the spotting system of the present day. It has always been true in every sport that as public competition develops, ways and means are constantly being sought, and found, to bring about steadily increasing improvement. The keenness of field trial competition stimulated the effort to show better and better dogs before the judges and the public. It was no longer enough merely to point and handle game. "The quality of the performance became more important than the frequency of the occurrence"—and thus handlers sought for greater speed, and wider range and more "class."

No longer were we content simply to let a dog go along at his own gait; but by both voice and whistle we began "pushing them out." Field trial dogs were not allowed to run for indefinite periods, but were always kept fresh and eager to go. This eagerness, coupled with the means employed to keep them out, led gradually to what we now know as bolters—which are nothing more or less than dogs which do not handle kindly and run away at every good opportunity. Dave Rose once said: "A field trial dog is one that runs away but not quite;" and in the theory that led to that statement lies the reason we have bolters to-day.

No one wants a dog that is constantly pottering around under his handler's feet; and no one wants a dog that is perpetually backcasting—for backcasting is simply lost motion and wasted time which accomplishes no good purpose. Therefore, to break a dog of backcasting, handlers would throw things at him to turn him out again. A barrage of pebbles, sticks or stones proved to be a good corrective measure, aided by the voice and whistle. Some even used "nigger shooters" to touch the dog up a bit and head him out. Thus our dogs were encouraged to *stay away* from their handlers when in the field, and the effort required to accomplish this in some instances had to be so forceful that it soon became the dog's real desire to stay away. That is when we began first to get our bolters.

Another thing that tended toward an increase of bolting inclinations was the system of *teaching a dog to run before teaching him to point.* This first came about with the advent of derby stakes; and has been further encouraged by the increasing number of spring puppy trials throughout the country. The plan of first teaching a dog to run and hunt game which he is allowed to flush, and placing him on "class" in the puppy and early derby stakes, means that pretty severe measures are often required when we later turn right about face and endeavor to teach this same dog to handle game stanchly. The severity of these measures as required at times is pretty apt to encourage an inclination to bolt. The dog decides in his own canine mind that he can have a much better time if he goes out on a hunting expedition of his own and forgets about his handler. If he is a kennel raised dog, lacking the bond of intimate companionship, he comes to feel that it is finer and freer just to do his hunting without the handicap of any sort of handler or restraint.

Like reproduces like often enough so that, in time, we came to have more and more dogs that had inherited tendencies toward self-hunting—or bolting. As field trials gave us constantly keener dogs, and as only the keenest of these were bred to, we developed dogs which inherited almost a mania for hunting; and this passion was so hard to keep in control that, in many cases, bolting followed as surely as "C" follows "B" in the alphabet.

There is a vast difference between the true bolter—the dog that really *desires* to get away—and the dog that simply goes so wide that his chances are increased of being lost on point. Many very wide dogs handle kindly and they are never to be classed as bolters even though they may at times become lost when handling game. Some dogs are so carried away by their enthusiasm for the hunt that they sometimes get out of hand—yet many of these are not truly to be classed as bolters. The dog that is a real bolter is the one that deliberately runs away on the first cast, or sneaks away at the first good opportunity. There are dogs that will actually make a deliberate effort to put a gully or hill or heavy cover between them and their handler in order that they may pass out of the picture. Some dogs are so clever in doing this that they continue to fool even their handlers that this is their deliberate intention.

In spite of the fact that we must charge field trial training with having given us the class of dogs known as bolters, we are firm in our belief that this is simply one of the penalties which must be paid for having accomplished a worth-while result on the whole. To compensate for the few bolters, we have improved the breeds in the main and have increased the hunting instinct, the passion for finding game. The end justifies the means and we can forgive our bolters in view of the greater good.

The other side of the picture is that one of the best cures for bolting is to get close to the dog and *develop his companionship.* Many dogs that have been confirmed bolters when keyed up to field trial competition, have given up their bolting entirely when hunting to the gun. This was true of the setter, Cæsar. The story is told of Cæsar that he once bolted the course in a field trial, to be found later that same day hunting kindly to the gun for some boys with whom he had fallen in company. Prince Rodney, too, became a dependable grouse dog in Michigan when hunted by his owner after his field trial career was over.

No matter what kind of a dog we have, the chances are that, if he is made a companion, and started right out from puppyhood to be handled and taught to the gun, he will not become a bolter if continued along these same lines. Yet he may be a keener and better bird dog than his ancestors were; and for that we may thank the field trial competitions—not to mention the fact that field trials are as fine a sport as can be found anywhere on earth.

There is no doubt about the pleasure of puppy trials. Those of us who love the game simply can't get enough of it. The same thing is true of derby stakes. It is a grave question, however, whether we might not to-day have better mannered dogs on game if there were no puppy stakes or derbies—particularly the former. Then we might just reverse the system of training and break a dog on game before teaching him to handle under field trial whistle signals. We could then make a gun dog of him first, and widen him out later on. We would thus always know that our dog will handle game—and that is something handlers are not now always sufficiently sure of even in All-Age stakes.

With the fundamental of handling game firmly and deeply implanted, we could take this same dog and later gradually key him up to field trial speed and range without so much danger of his forgetting his early training in the fundamentals. But under the present system of teaching a dog to run and hunt first, hoping later on to bring him down to handling game, we are always running the risk of not being able to accomplish this purpose without harmful results such as bolting and sometimes blinking.

Inasmuch as it was the desire for more speed and more range and more "class" that led to some of our dogs becoming bolters, suppose we discuss this subject of speed and range for a few minutes. *Both are purely relative.* The fastest Bird Dog is slow by comparison to the Greyhound; and what might be considered wide range in grouse country would look mighty cramped on the prairies of Manitoba or the open quail country of the South.

The thing that stimulates speed and that leads to range is a desire to find birds. The keener this desire the greater will be the speed within the limits of each dog's capability. In like manner, if a dog whose hunting instinct is keen does not find birds close at hand, he will keep reaching on out farther and farther in his desire to find them. We are not speaking of the "whistle runners," whose speed and range have been artificially developed, but of those dogs whose speed and range are natural.

It is surprising how ideas vary with respect to speed and range. Many people have asked the writer to see their dogs in the field, which dogs they have boasted of as fast, wide rangers. Unless such people have ever seen a really wide dog, I always know the chances are a hundred to one against seeing anything worth while. I have almost invariably found it so. Only the past season a man asked me to see what he thought was a prospect for the puppy trials. He claimed the dog was too wide for shooting and was debating whether to slow him down and shorten him up for shooting, or to let him go and enter him in the competitions. The description was so glowing that I thought I would at least see a halfway prospect. What I did see, when we got in the field, was a dog without enough go in him to hunt grouse even in the closest cover.

Last fall I had the pleasure of shooting on two or three occasions with a friend who had just gotten a new English Setter bitch. She was a very comfortable little shooting dog.

She was not fast, nor was she wide; but she was above the average and wide enough for hunting afoot. The other day this same man was telling me about his dog and explained that he hoped to get her to work a little closer to the gun this season. *Yet she wasn't any too wide last fall*—just barely wide enough!

A level-headed dog will adjust his range and speed to fit the country he is hunting. A brainy dog will go wider when you are on horseback than he will when you are afoot. Such a dog will go wider in open country than he will in close country. Alford's John was a dog of that type. There was never any danger of losing old John. Yet he was wide enough to be the greatest field trial dog of his day. Hunting for his owner on foot, however, the only chance to lose John was to lose him on point. Otherwise, he would look you up, for he always charged himself with the responsibility of keeping in touch with the gun.

Mohawk II, also, was just such a practical dog, although he ranked with Sioux as the two greatest field trial dogs of their day. Sioux was still another of the same stripe, and she once won a heavy wager for her owner when she was hunted all day long against several shooting dogs and found more birds than all of them. Jim Avent has always claimed that Sioux was the greatest dog or bitch he ever saw or handled. Seaview Rex, of the present day, is a pointer of similar qualifications, as is also the triple National Champion, Becky Broomhill.

Many will tell you that a field trial dog never makes a good shooting dog. That all depends. If one is hunting from horseback in the South, there is no question but that a high grade field trial dog is the ideal shooting dog. If hunting afoot in closer country, it depends a great deal upon the brains and adaptability of the dog—and how biddable he is. A wild, wide ranger that is hard to handle will be too much of a bother for the shooter to enjoy his hunt and handle his dog at the same time; but the dog that merely goes wide in his search for game, hunting all the likely cover and yet not passing up birdy places near at hand—the dog that will swing kindly to hand or whistle—there you have the ideal shooting companion. Such a dog is almost certain to find infinitely more game than the kind of canine that simply potters around a few feet in front of the hunter. Even the grouse dog should go wide enough to find game, or you might just as well not have a dog.

Ray Holland, the Editor of *Field & Stream,* had an ideal grouse dog in his pointer named Bob, which has recently passed on to the Great Beyond. Bob was always hunted on grouse with a bell attached to his collar. He was the type of dog whose range, had he been hunted even on the prairies, would have adjusted itself accordingly. But most of his experience was on grouse, and although perhaps wider than the average grouse dog, he represented the ideal; and it is the writer's belief that the very close dogs do not.

The effort to breed dogs with lots of "fire" gave us, in some instances, what the late C. B. Whitford used to call "mechanical insanity." Many of these became bolters. Lots of fire is what we want in our Bird Dogs if it can be coupled with level-headedness. It is possible to breed dogs thus well balanced, even though in the process some of them may degenerate into bolters. It is better even to have some bolters, and separate the wheat from the chaff, than it would be to breed only from the phlegmatic kind and end up finally by having dogs without enough intense hunting interest to go anywhere.

It is true that on occasion dogs may become bolters later in life, when keyed up by field trial training and competition, even though in their younger days they may have handled more kindly. This, however, is rarer than the kind that never reach the stage where they can be broken. These may make winning puppies and derbies, but are never brought on to dependable pointing and all too often become bolters eventually. Yet after all is said and done, the average hunter can take most any kind of a dog and, coupling constant companionship with the right kind of training, develop him into a practical companion in the field. This is an entirely different situation than that presented to the field trial handler, who has a kennel of dogs. He can never come into such intimate contact with any one dog as the hunter does with his canine pal, to which he devotes his entire time and attention.

All hunters, however, can thank the field trial competitions for giving us, through selective breeding, dogs that average keener in their desire to find game than did most of the dogs our forefathers were accustomed to hunt over before field trials were heard of in America.

CHAPTER XII

BLINKERS

FUNDAMENTALLY, *blinking* is an outgrowth of the same general factors that lead to bolting, which was the subject of our discussion in the last chapter. It traces back directly to the development of dogs in which hunting instinct and energy have become the all-dominant desire. Such dogs never get enough of hunting—and they are never permitted to; the keen edge must never be dulled.

Gun dogs which spend days at a time afield with their masters should never become *blinkers;* and such dogs never will do any blinking if they are in good hands. An unreasonably harsh master, of course, may make a blinker out of most any dog. Such people should never own a dog. Unfortunately, they sometimes do; but, happily, these constitute the exception rather than the rule.

Blinking is nothing more nor less than a definite unwillingness to indicate the presence of birds. The word "definite" is used purposely. Blinking is not blinking if there be no definite intent. A dog may be off nose and fail to find birds that may be there—but that is not blinking in any sense of the word. Blinking is blinking only when birds are passed *intentionally.*

Blinking is not hereditary. It is a development that is most apt to make itself manifest when the "brakes" are applied too strenuously to a dog whose desire to find game exceeds the instinct to stop. Most of us like to let our puppies gather hunting experience before we attempt to stop them up on game. We like to let them learn to search with judgment before we deem it necessary to teach them stanchness on point. The first fundamental for a dog is to be useful in *finding* game. Otherwise, he is simply more or less of a "fifth wheel." We want our dogs to hunt wisely and well before we ask them to indicate their finds by pointing. This is but natural. Usually it proves the logical process.

Suppose, now, we just let ourselves imagine the situation that confronts us when this young dog, which up to a certain point has been permitted considerable freedom on his finds, is suddenly called upon to point game instead of flushing and chasing it. Here is a dog keyed up to the very *n*th degree of energy and hunting desire. He is all atremble in his ruling passion to seek the scent of game birds. He is a high-strung individual. His early hunts have been full of freedom and he is filled with an inherited fire.

There comes a time, however, when we must ask this dog to pass from puppyhood into manhood—to point game and point it stanchly. Yet we must not take away too much of the natural fire. This process demands very delicate handling. A happy balance must be preserved in achieving a dependable stanchness on point without losing too much, if any, of the passion to seek the delicious odor which game birds bring to a Bird Dog's delicate nose.

There you have in a nutshell the situation that so often results in blinkers. You can't come down on such a dog too rapidly or too hard. It must be a gradual process and as delicately tempered as the tuning of a musical instrument. In preceding discussions we have considered the art of teaching to point. If these instructions are properly followed, there will be no difficulty. We may have to wait a while on the good ones to come down to it—but they're worth waiting for. Take your time. Some day a situation will favor you so that you can get to your dog and get your hands on him. Then if you hold him on point and gently but firmly steady him, keeping him where he belongs and working with him so that he understands what he is intended to do, the ultimate goal will draw much nearer. Such favorable opportunities will then come oftener and the time will arrive when you can bank on your dog to be there with his birds, holding them fast and true, no matter how long it takes you to get to him.

But suppose, on the other hand, an ignorant and impatient handler were in charge of this same dog in the same situation. It is so easy for a man who doesn't truly understand canine nature to become impatient and overly anxious to bring about a quick result. The dog is naturally impetuous. He is punished for it. He is jerked into position instead of merely held to his position firmly. In short, it is possible to be so rough that the dog loses all of his inspired natural feelings of pleasure at finding birds. He comes to associate his finds with punishment. He decides that since his finds seem to lead only to punishment, the thing to do is cease to find. Not all of them, of course, reach exactly this reasoning—but many of them do and these are rapidly headed toward becoming confirmed blinkers.

A blinker, then, is a dog that simply dodges his birds. A blinker is perhaps the most useless of any Bird Dog. Almost any fault can be easier forgiven than blinking—which makes it all the more deplorable that *blinking is usually some man's fault.* You may, perhaps justifiably, blame the dog which doesn't show early pointing instinct and develop rapidly. But, condemn this as you may, you can always know that he would at least never blink if properly handled. You can say almost anything else about him—but not that. The fellow who is not willing to take his time with such a dog had better sell him and get another one. Someone may thus some day get a real one that might otherwise become a blinker.

The reason blinking is such a serious fault is that the really crafty blinker will learn to cheat you even out of the knowledge that he is blinking. Experienced dog men can often detect by a dog's actions whether or not there is any ground for suspicions of blinking, but the novice handler usually misses these.

Some blinkers, which have not yet been entirely cowed, may point birds indecisively for a minute or two and then sneak away from them. Others have been so cowed that they fear even to get near the birds and circle them at the first scent of their presence. But the true blinker never flushes birds. The severity of his punishment has taught him the danger of that. Blinking is an aftermath of punishment so severe that a dog comes even to fear the very presence of birds. He used to love to find them but now he fears the consequences. Some dogs may be so hard-headed that they will stand a lot of punishment and still not become stanch on point for a long time. But flushing is not blinking in any sense of the word. If you are in sight of your dog, you know if he flushes birds; but you may never know it if he is blinking them. That is why the latter is so insidious.

Be very careful in bringing your dog through the stage when the tendency to blink is most apt to crop out. If you notice that your attempt to control the natural desire to flush is causing your dog to become timid on his points—*go easy with him.* What you do at this stage will be the making or breaking of him. Get him past the danger stage and you will be all right. Temper your control with enough encouragement so that he hunts happily and without the shadow of a doubt dulling the keenness of his desire.

There are usually exceptions to all rules. Perhaps there are blinkers which have developed the fault for some reason other than the manhandling to which I have attributed it. But I doubt this. Nevertheless, some will claim that certain timid dogs become blinkers because they are frightened by the sudden noise of a flushing covey. Others state that some dogs, especially those that have been permitted to do a good deal of self-hunting, may get into the habit of finding one covey and then leaving these birds to go on and make another find. Various degrees and types of blinkers are discussed. But the present writer is "from Missouri" and will have to be shown before he believes that blinking very often, if ever, comes from any other reason than that we have assigned as its cause.

I can understand how blinking might be closely associated with gun-shyness. I think, in fact, that I know of one instance where the two faults blended pretty much into one. This was the case of a Pointer derby that was a big field trial winner and pretty well finished on his game for a young dog. One day his owner took him out for a hunt with some companions and several guns were fired simultaneously over his first find. This sudden cannonading was so unexpected that the dog went to his next covey more timidly. When the bombardment was repeated, he developed a sudden and very aggravated case of gun-shyness. Before his owner realized what was happening, the dog went a step farther and began to blink his birds—evidently fearing that to stay on point would bring the dreaded guns into play. Yes, there may be rare exceptions to the rule I have laid down, but exceptions only serve to prove the rule. And, even in the case I have mentioned, the fault of gun-shyness was so closely associated with the blinking, that it is hard to separate the two.

Nine times out of ten the blinker will be too hard to cure to be worth bothering about —and only a master in the art of handling should attempt it with hope of success. If the dog is otherwise an exceptional specimen, he will be worth saving. Usually his days of usefulness are over and a home should be found for him as a family pet. Blinking can be cured, however, just as most any canine fault can—but this calls for pains and patience. It cannot be accomplished quickly.

To cure a blinker, I should hunt the faulty dog with a true one. When the true dog finds birds, bring up your blinker and give him a smell of them too. Encourage him in pointing them until he sees there is nothing to fear. Hold him gently but firmly to the point and stroke him, speaking words of encouragement. By having your hands on him you can prevent him from moving either forward or backward. By this process of quiet encouragement, you will let him know that everything is all right. Then have a companion step in and flush the bevy, while you speak quietly to the dog as the birds take wing—"steady boy!" Repeat this performance several times; and then have your companion kill a bird. Have him bring this bird to your pupil, while you still have your hands on him. Let the dog smell the dead bird and put his mouth on it. Do all that you can to make it absolutely clear that all is well. It will take time to effect a permanent cure—but then all true training takes time. It takes, in fact, more time than the average novice imagines.

My friend who owned the Pointer just referred to had to break his dog of the blinking before he attempted to cure him of gun-shyness. The dog had become afraid to go to his birds and so something had to be done to destroy this fear. My friend used an old tried and true gun dog that he didn't fear to spoil, and, when this dog found birds, he would rush in and flush them, calling the blinker to follow, encouraging him to join in the flush and chase. Thus he made it clear to the dog that there was nothing to fear. The result was that the dog gradually began again to take an active interest in finding game and flushing and chasing it. Thus was the blinking cured. Of course, later he had to be steadied all over again. But thus was he cured of the worst fault a Bird Dog can have.

And lastly, he had to be cured of the gun-shyness. It made a double dose of extra work for his master, but this particular dog happened to be worth it. Furthermore, it was not the dog's fault—but the fault of his master—that he ever developed either fault. No man has any business to invite an army of guns to shoot over a young dog. Two guns are enough to shoot even over an old dog—and one is all that should ever be shot over a young dog until there is absolutely no question from any standpoint as to what the answer will be.

I have discussed the cause of blinking and also hinted at a possible cure for the few that are worth attempting to cure. I will conclude by repeating that there will be small need to think or know anything about blinkers if dogs are handled properly. There is no reason or excuse for dogs that point quite naturally at an early age ever to become blinkers; and there is never but very little likelihood that the phlegmatic kind will be given cause to develop blinking inclinations. On the other hand, if you have a dog with such a highly developed passion for hunting that he does not relish restraint, be mighty careful in your handling of him when you become impatient at his failure to point and hold his birds. Better go a little easier and a little slower and have a real one in the end, rather than attempt to speed up the process and run the chance of ending up with a blinker.

One type of blinking that should perhaps be mentioned before concluding this chapter—a somewhat less aggravated type—has to do with the circler or shifter. What we naturally want our dogs to do is to go boldly to their birds and point them steadily as soon as the scent is "right." Some dogs, however, get into bad habits. Dogs that have often been lost on point—or that may have been permitted to indulge in an excess of self-hunting—these are the ones most likely to become circlers or shifters. In the former case, the failure of the handler to arrive and flush the birds—and in the latter case, the lack of any handler at all—leads to the dog soon taking liberty with his manners. He gets restless holding those birds that are not flushed for him—and this restlessness causes him to circle and shift, which is nothing more nor less than moving about and testing the scent from different angles.

When this fault (one form of blinking) is discovered, the handler should work with the dog the next time he points. Get to him and steady him with your hands. Lift him gently by the tail. Press forward from the rear—which will steady him. Exercise a little of both care and common sense and you should soon overcome this mild form of blinking. But cut out any more chances for the dog to go self-hunting; and double up on your efforts to keep him from getting lost on point in the future.

CHAPTER XIII

SUGGESTIONS ON HANDLING

DON'T make the mistake of hacking your dog. Give him his head. When you know that he is broken—so that you may trust him on game—let him develop independence of judgment in finding it. No phase of hunting is more fascinating than the privilege of watching a good dog exercise keen initiative in his plans and method of search.

An error that is far too common among hunters is to suppose that the dog is performing best when he is hunting within a stone's throw of the gun. Those of this belief are prone to keep calling to the dog to bring him in. They feel that if he is out of sight for a few minutes, everything is all wrong. Nothing could be farther from the truth.

How can a dog concentrate his mind and his efforts on finding game if he is being constantly diverted and hacked by a restless master? If you are forever ordering the dog this way and that, he cannot possibly attend properly to his job. He knows as much about finding game as you do—and nine times out of ten he knows more. You can't help him much. So why try? Give him his head. It's apt to be a wiser head than yours in his particular sphere. And if it isn't, he won't be of much help to you anyhow.

In certain types of country a dog can scarcely go too wide—provided he handles. On the other hand, it is easily possible for a dog to work too close to be of any value. The brainy dog will adapt his range to the class of the country. If you own that kind of dog, leave it to him. Give him the freedom to do his job well. Don't worry so much about him—for that only leads to your worrying him.

Encourage your dog to hunt merrily. Hacking him merely discourages it. Be glad to see your dog go to his birds with a high head for the body scent. Hacking leads to foot-scenting potterers. The broken dog knows what he is about and what it is his job to do. Don't keep him from doing it. Give him his head and thus a chance to do that job well. It is assumed, of course, that we are speaking of the finished performer.

Your dog should be biddable. That is to be expected. If you call him in to seek dead birds and retrieve, that is one thing. So also if you have marked down a single that the dog's eye may have missed. It should be manifest that what we have said refers to the kind of hacking that is unjustified by any situation. We are not referring to the special cases where orders are necessary. What we do abhor is a perpetual outflow of distracting commands that simply divert the dog's attention without having any mission to accomplish. *The prettiest performances are pursued in silence.* A shouting hunter spoils his own day.

The dog should work out in front, to the sides and ahead. Backcasting is hunting in the wrong direction. But backcasting should be cured before the hunt—not during it. Get your dogs ready *ahead of time.* Don't expect them to perform properly and pleasingly if you have been too busy, too careless or too lazy to get them ready *before the hunting season.* And this has reference to *condition* as well as *manners.* Proper preparation is the big thing. If you have not prepared for pleasure—be prepared for disappointment.

We can begin to work our Bird Dogs in the field along the latter part of August. The young quail, pheasants and other game birds will be far enough along (except a few late hatches) so that they will be able to fly and a dog can be worked on them with perfect impunity.

Midday in August will still be too hot in most sections of the country, but the days are long at this time of year and daylight will continue for a sufficient length of time during the cool of the evening to make it possible to have a lot of fun with our dogs after eating the evening meal, especially if fields are handy where game abides. Nothing can be accomplished until after the grain is cut, but this will be the general condition at the time of which we speak.

A good run in the cool of such evenings, for not to exceed thirty minutes, will begin gradually the hardening process of getting your dog ready for the fall hunting season after the long inactivity of the summer months. It is a pity that everyone doesn't do this. It is not fair to a dog to start hunting him in the fall without proper conditioning; and you will be more than repaid if you do harden your hunting companion against his later days afield, for the work delivered will be of infinitely higher class than could otherwise be possible.

The natural tendency of most dogs is to hunt out ahead. It should be easy to teach yours to swing to a motion of the arm. Suppose you want him to swing to the right. You wave your arm in that direction. If the dog does not at once respond, turn yourself and walk in the direction indicated, continuing to motion him with the arm. If he still fails to take heed, *start to run*—and the chances are ten to one this will draw the dog that way also. He thinks something important is about to transpire, and he wants to be in on it. Thus you have accomplished your purpose and turned him. In time you will be able to swing him by the arm signal alone.

When you have finally perfected your dog in always swinging *out* on his casts, you have very materially reduced the chances of losing him, even though he may go wide. You have eliminated backcasting—and that cuts in half the amount of territory in which he might go astray. If you will but quiet your restlessness, the chances are eight in ten that the dog will soon be in vision again, even though he may be out of sight for a few minutes in heavy cover. But if such does not prove to be the case, then it is time to look him up. Simply go to the place where you last saw him and begin from there to try and figure out where he should be. If you use good judgment in following the likely looking cover, the chances are your dog will be there somewhere with his birds. There's nothing to get excited over. And you won't think clearly if you do. So keep your head.

If your dog is lost on point, don't manifest impatience while trying to locate him. He is but doing his duty—and very likely doing it well—so don't disturb his trust in you, and even cause him to doubt himself, by shouting at him roughly, simply because you don't happen to know for the moment just where he is.

The whistle signals are always of value in

handling a wide dog while hunting. A prolonged whistle is to bring him in. A short, sharp single whistle is to let him know where you are or to check him up for orders if he is in sight, then you can wave him as desired. The sharp, short double note is to send him on wider than he is already working. Drill your dog well in these whistle signals. They will save your voice—are not so disturbing to game as the human lungs—and can be heard much farther.

The writer recently spent a short time in New England and had with him a field trial winner on both quail and pheasants. An ardent local hunter invited me to go afield with him. We took both my dog and his. The hill country and cover were new to mine and she didn't start out so well. I gave her the short double whistle signal, and it rang out sharp and clear. My friend asked me what it meant. I told him the bitch was going so poorly that I wanted to urge her on. This surprised him for he told me she was already hunting too far from us.

To his own dog he kept whistling constantly—*to keep him in!* Yet the dog never got out of "spitting range." Soon we came to a draw, bordered by a heavy thicket. Here his dog began to flush a few pheasants, much as a Spaniel would perform. I began looking for my bitch—and soon found her *on point.* She had three birds "locked up tight." Other quick, high-headed, body scent points followed in rapid succession. I could have killed four times the limit in ten minutes—if I had hit them—all over positive points. My friend was won over then and there.

Yes, as I said in the beginning, *don't make the mistake of hacking your dog.* When you know he is broken dependably, give him his head. You'll end up by having happier hunts, and will bag your birds with many more thrills.

We have all often heard that "not all is gold that glitters." The same is true in connection with the performances of dogs. I have just had some correspondence with a man who wrote me about what he thought was a remarkable performance. But after getting my letter of contrary comment, he frankly acknowledged that he saw my point of contention. Without further comment, I am introducing these letters to speak for themselves, and you may draw your own conclusions:

First Letter from My Correspondent

"Last week I went over to see an old dog man who lives near me. He is a New Englander who is as fine a handler of dogs as any man could wish for. We took one of his dogs out into a large open field near his home. My friend waited until the dog was about a hundred yards away—when he whistled twice. The dog turned instantly and started to work back toward us. My friend next raised his hand above his head and swung it off toward the right. The dog swung in that direction like a piece of well-oiled machinery. Then the old fellow raised his hand above his head again, and this time brought it down quickly toward the ground and yelled 'sh-h-h-h-h-h!' This time the dog instantly dropped flat in his tracks. I thought you might like to hear about this performance, which was as pretty a sight as I can ever recall."

And This Was My Reply

"That must, as you say, have been a pretty piece of work. The thought runs through my mind, however, that such tactics would have a natural tendency to take away some of the dog's own initiative. Our American complaint of most English dogs is that they are 'over-broken.' Some of us in America may sometimes be guilty of working dogs that are what might be termed 'under-broken.' Perhaps there is a happy medium lying between the two—at least the present writer has always so thought regarding the matter.

"The fact remains, however, that what a dog will learn to do on his own initiative seems to be more really worth while and more fraught with interest, than that which he may merely be taught to do. I, myself, am always interested in seeing my dogs *think things out.* I don't like to dominate the situation too much myself—just keep a subtle influence ever present, which makes for harmony of purpose between dog and handler. The display of a developed brain is always more interesting than any performance which might be on the border line of a parlor trick.

"At least in the case of my favorite dog, I am positive I could make her duplicate the performance you have described—but I wouldn't do it, even though I know that I could. It would simply lead to her soon losing a certain amount of her own initiative and independence of action—and that would mean a greater loss than could ever be replaced by a purely mechanical control."

Second Letter from My Correspondent

"Your letter is very interesting to me. Although I have had a dog since I was old enough to lift one, I can by no means claim to be an authority on handling them. Consequently, the criticism in your letter has been a very helpful one to me.

"Your point, that a dog can have his initiative taken away, is a very good one for me to bear in mind. It has brought home to me the fact that, after all, a man depends upon his dog a great deal. If, on the other hand, the dog is depending upon the man, it seems logical to believe that the hunter's pockets are not so apt to bulge with game."

All of which is very true.

CHAPTER XIV

"BUSINESS" DOGS

THE reader may undoubtedly have gathered the impression, and correctly, that the present writer's distinct preference in a Bird Dog is for one that will reach out and go to his game. Keen and intelligent search are so very essential! The dog that potters around with semi-indifference, always almost "close enough to spit on," isn't going to find very much game that a hunter wouldn't walk up anyhow. That being the case, a Spaniel would be about as valuable as a Setter or Pointer—in which case the art of handling game by pointing loses relatively a lot of its importance. But there are exceptions to all rules and it may be interesting to discuss some of these exceptions.

During the past season, I had the privilege of shooting over a couple of Bird Dogs that I would classify as "business" fellows. These dogs would deliver about as much game to the gun as most any Pointer or Setter one might hope to find. Yet their hunting characteristics were so distinctive as to lead themselves to a special discussion.

One of these dogs was a Pointer named Sport, owned by Mr. Whit Cook down in Mississippi. I had the pleasure of shooting over this dog on several occasions and found him to be unique in that he was a remarkably good covey dog, without having many of the characteristics that would commend him to field trial judges, at least in certain types of territory. The unique thing about this is that the average field trial dog is apt to shine more as a covey finder than on singles. Yet Sport was just a plain, practical purpose dog —a *"business"* dog.

You could start out on a hunt with Sport and he was good to go all day, every day. Yet he would go in his own way. If he didn't think there were birds about, he might trot along in close proximity to the horses. Thus he rested and conserved his strength and energy. At no time was Sport fast. Yet I have seen him bore out into likely looking cover as far as any field trial dog that ever ran and could still be handled. And usually when Sport went out on one of these long casts, you could bet on him ending up with a covey find. After that, he might go right out again on another cast—if he had an idea that results might be produced thereby—or he might trot along close to the horses for a while, when he would feel that a long cast in any special territory might prove barren of results.

I have wondered whether Sport would hunt strange territory with similarly effective results. I am inclined to believe that down in his own country he had every one of those coveys marked and numbered—and just went to them one after another in their numerical order. In other words, to a certain extent, Sport may have done his hunting somewhat from memory. Unquestionably his familiarity with the territory over which he hunted, and with the birds therein, did help him a lot.

But still I am inclined to believe that Sport would have made a fairly good showing in any territory. He was the kind of dog that does not fear to go to his birds. He hunted with splendid independence—and independence is *so* valuable when susceptible to control. One afternoon I saw Sport find eleven coveys against a blank score for two bracemates—yet one of those bracemates showed every qualification that Sport lacked, except bird-finding ability. The answer is that, after all is said and done, we've got to take off our hats to the "business" dogs. It might merely be added further, that no dog will ever prove a real "business" dog if he doesn't ever range out and cover his ground. Besides which, such dogs have usually learned *how* to make the best use of a superlatively good nose.

Another "business" dog that I have recently seen is a very large Setter. This dog would not have a ghost of a chance to win a place in the average field trial. Yet, even though it may seem almost as a contradiction, this dog is bold and independent—with a world of style on game.

But he hasn't the slightest spark of competitive spirit. He just goes out and struts his stuff without ever a care as to the performance of a bracemate. His bracemate is totally ignored and this big Setter simply goes about his business in a businesslike way. He will bore out into good cover as wide and as fast as any dog need go to win a field trial. Yet he won't cross barren ground to get to cover—until his master gets there also. Across open stretches he will simply trot along socially like a cordial and companionable house dog. Yet, when he strikes cover—oh boy!

This dog's master knows that he could win field trials if it were not for this failing. He has tried in every possible way to interest the dog in putting on his hunts regardless. All to no avail. The dog simply looks up with those great big, soulful eyes of his and seems to say: "What's the use? Let's go on over to the cover *together.* What's the hurry? I'll get there as soon as you will—and there is no use in my getting there first. I don't want to find birds and just stand there until you find me—I'm a *'business'* dog. So let's just go on and stroll along together, master, and then when *both* of us hit cover—I'll bore out and find your birds."

I believe that somewhat of the above thoughts are actually what goes through this dog's mind. He says so with his eyes and with his actions, even if he lacks the words. And yet I have seen this dog go through a morning with two bracemates, either of which could beat him in a field trial—yet there have been occasions when I have seen this big Setter find every covey shot to in the course of a half day's hunt. Of course he has a *marvelous* nose. All "business" dogs *must* have—or they would do no business.

Just very recently I saw an exemplification of the characteristics of this dog. We had him out with a field trial winner. We came to a great wide stretch of good cover and those two dogs cut up that territory as attractively as any dogs I have ever seen could do it. My friend said: "Look at that big devil way out there—that's style and range for you!"

And the truth of the matter is that the big Setter *was* out just as far as his bracemate, hunting just as well and with as much style and speed. Then both dogs swung over a hill in the distance and made a backcast taking in some territory behind the woods to the left. Soon they came in sight of us again—and right then was when the difference between them became strikingly manifest.

The little bitch cut right back out ahead again and rechecked the territory with the same speed, style and animation as before. It is true that she hunted down the field farther to the right than on her original cast. Yet the fact remains, and must be admitted, that she came pretty close to rehunting the same field a second time.

The big dog, in the meantime, came over and joined my friend and myself. Together the three of us went down through that field. The big dog looked up at us as much as to say: "Well, friends, that little bitch and I put on a great hunt through here—it's too bad we didn't strike birds—but they're not in here to-day. It's a lovely day, though, isn't it?" And so the three of us strolled along side by side. You couldn't have moved the big dog with dynamite—until we came to an entirely new stretch of cover on ahead. Then the big dog bored out again into the cover.

But here's a strange thing—when that big

dog hunts a field and then comes back for a stroll with you, it's dollars to doughnuts that no other dog will go in that field and find birds behind him. The little bitch didn't on the occasion just mentioned. Had she done so, I should charge the big Setter more severely than I can now do. You can't get an awful lot of thrill or kick out of some of these "business" dogs when they are in their more sociable moods—but, even at that, you've got to take off your hat to them when they hunt in their own way and don't give any other dog a chance to pick up birds that they have missed. If they don't like a territory and figure it doesn't contain birds and hence is not worth hunting—or if they have hunted the territory and won't recheck it—if on occasion they just saunter along with us as if on dress parade—we can't blame them quite so much as we otherwise might, when the check-up at the end of the day's hunt shows that they have not been out-birded by their bracemates.

There are, here and there, these dogs of a strictly practical type, and such as these will furnish any man a real day afield. But be not misled—it is not the sauntering habits of these dogs that is to commend them—but their commendable traits which make them valuable. Without their commendable characteristics they would be valueless. Therefore, don't mistake as a "business" dog one that simply has the failings—but lacks their good points. For their faults we can forgive them because of their other merits—yet without those other merits we could not forgive their faults.

CHAPTER XV

FIELD TRIAL IDEALS *vs.* SHOOTING CONCEPTIONS

IN THE fifth brace of the All-Age stake at a recent field trial, four opposites were brought into direct competition. Two of these were the dogs involved; and the other two were their handlers. One of the dogs was a well-bred Pointer which had been shot to in the field for several seasons, but which had never before faced the judges and gallery in a field trial. His bracemate was a Setter bitch that also had seen several seasons of hard service in front of the gun, in addition to which this dog had accumulated some dozen field trial wins in fast company.

About the same difference marked their respective handlers. The owner of the Pointer was seeing his first field trial, while the Setter was being piloted by the same man who had handled her in every one of her wins. To these two it was an old story. They understood each other; and each understood what kind of a performance was called for to meet field trial standards.

When the judges gave the order to let them go, the Setter bitch went away like a blue streak, but her owner settled himself in his saddle with a confidence born of many campaigns, knowing full well that his charge could be handled like the proverbial glove, no matter how wide she might go, just so long as a signal could reach her. The Pointer, in the meantime, ambled along a short distance ahead of his handler's horse. He may never have seen his master mounted before, and this may have confused him—or it may be that he had simply been developed along close lines.

Toward the close of the heat, however, this Pointer stumbled upon a bevy of birds and handled them perfectly. He was steady to shot and wing and had his birds accurately located. A few minutes later his owner pulled his horse over near that of his competitor and, almost trembling with excitement, whispered: "D'you think they'll place him?"

"No," came the answer from the other

handler who had been through the mill.

The fond owner was crestfallen, but came right back with another question: "D'you think he'll make a field trial dog?"

And again the answer was: "No."

You see it is not the find alone that counts—but the work that has led to the find. Was it the result of diligent *search?* Was it brought about as the climax of an *intelligent cast?* Was it a find that called for superlative *nose?* Was it a mere accident—or a just *reward* for well-directed effort? Was the dog *fast* and *attractive* in action, both going to his game and on it?

Those are questions that field trial judges want to see answered when any dog finds game. It is an old axiom of field trials that: "The *quality* of the performance is of greater moment than the mere frequency of the occurrence." The truly high-class performance is the very acme of *art.*

Yet—lest any of our readers may misunderstand—let me add that the Setter bitch that beat this Pointer is herself a gun dog in every sense of the word. And she could beat him under any standard of judgment,

A Spectacular Find—the Kind That Will Win Field Trials

day in and day out, long heats or short, week after week. She is shot over regularly on quail, pheasants and Hungarians; and she "does it all," from the matchless find to the delicate delivery of the dead bird. For after all is said and done—and all beliefs to the contrary notwithstanding—the *ideal* field trial dog is the gun dog of your dreams. Notice I used the word "ideal." Not all field trial competitors fulfill the meaning of the word; hence not all of them would make good gun dogs.

The greatest of our field trial winners, however, have been the most faultless gun dogs. Such a list would include Champion Doughboy; Champion Becky Broomhill; Champion Sioux; Champion Alford's John; Champion Candy Kid; Champion Mohawk II; Champion Seaview Rex; and many others. So if you ever hear anyone venture the assertion that field trial winners are no good as gun dogs you may just set it down that he has told either only half the story—or *doesn't know*.

At another recent field trial a situation occurred that brought out what is perhaps a somewhat common misunderstanding of field trial conceptions by the fellow whose days afield have been exclusively on shooting trips. A splendid brace was in action, again a Pointer and a Setter. They both cut out the country fast, wide and stylishly. Either of them is excellent on game; and both have been shot over heavily. In this case both handlers, too, were men of wide experience both in the hunting field and at the competitions—men who know that a field trial is a race to beat your bracemate to the birds.

Although both dogs had been working with the utmost independence, when the heat was about half over they chanced to draw together for a short stretch as they raced for a certain likely looking piece of cover that lay ahead. As it later turned out, they both passed dangerously close to a bevy that it seemed as if one or both of them should have nailed. One of the horsemen in the gallery flushed this bevy a short distance to the left of where the dogs had passed. The birds settled on ahead in the cover toward which the dogs were heading, and both handlers were keen to try for the singles as each knew that a point would mean that both dogs would place at the top of the stake. Usually a find on marked singles is far below a bevy find in the eyes of the judges, and justly so—but in this case no bird work up to this time had been coupled to a sufficiently good all-around performance to be classed with these two dogs should either or both of them handle game, even though it might be but a single bird.

We whipped through the cover where the birds had settled and in a short time the Setter was on game. His find proved to be two birds and he was steady as the proverbial rock. The Pointer, though she worked industriously, failed to connect with game—and the one find was all the Setter scored. The cover was whipped through twice—and then we all moved on. The Setter won the stake. The good Pointer did not place. At another time the tables might easily have been reversed—for either of those dogs can beat the other, all depending on which one gets the breaks on any given occasion.

The next day a friend of mine who had

seen the event came into my office and asked me for my version of the affair.

"Why didn't Mr. Jones (that's not his name) keep his Pointer bitch in that cover until she had located a bird? We all knew that more were still in there somewhere," he said.

"You miss the point of the thing," I replied. "I admit that in that cover those birds were hard to pick up. And yet the bitch had gone through it twice and failed. To have pottered around there any longer would have got her nowhere, even had she found after her third attempt. Her owner well knew this, and that's why he sent her on. He still had a gambler's chance for a bevy find and this would win the stake, where a delayed find on a single would win nothing at all. The idea of field trials is not to potter around in one place until a point is finally produced. The idea is speed and style and snap. If that is lacking, all is lacking. It isn't just the point alone that counts, you see—it's the *class* with which it is done. The Pointer bitch might just as well not find at all unless she could find quickly."

"I see," he said—but I still somewhat doubt if he really did.

In this great sport of Field Trials, as in any other game, one must take the breaks as they come—must accept the bitter with the sweet—and there will be plenty of both for those who stick. The whole world hates a quitter and the present writer knows of nothing sadder than to see some potential field trial fan finally drop out when his dogs are not winning. Be a glutton for punishment and come back for more of it—still smiling—and with constantly better dogs. The game needs this kind of true sportsmen; but has no use for the quitters. It is never a disgrace to be beaten fairly, in any sport. Nor is it in field trials; and all old-timers know this. They have all been beaten often, but they have always come back for more. And the world loves a good loser. It always will.

Remember this—that field trial men see a hundred dogs to every one the mere shooter sees. Therefore, it is but fair to assume that the former class, as a pretty general rule, knows more about them. If you go into the game—and I assure you it is a great one—go into it to *learn.* You will be repaid manyfold—for some day, as surely as the sunrise at dawn, you will land an entry among the winners, if you will but profit by the opportunity for a broadened experience with the canine kind. And when the thrill of your first win surges through your very soul, it will mean many, many times more to you than any mere private shoot can ever possibly mean. The latter may some day begin to pass from the picture; but the vivid memory of your first field trial win never will fade.

Let me close with an illustrative story. A friend of mine was handling his wonderfully good Pointer in a stake that anyone would glory to win. The dog made a magnificent find and stood up to his birds with superb style. His handler was manifestly excited when he went forward to flush. He put up a great big bevy, and the dog was steady. We all knew then that he had the stake at his mercy.

That evening my friend was telling me about it and he said: "You saw the bird, didn't you?"

"What bird?" I asked.

"Why, the one I flushed to that point this afternoon."

Then I realized how far my friend's excitement had carried him. The bevy had contained at least twenty birds and everyone had seen them all, except the dog's fond handler! To him they had all merged into one. But it didn't matter, for he had won the stake—a win he will never forget.

Some of us were smiling about it later and one of the party spoke up: "Pshaw, that's nothing," he said. "Why, last January when Jack Carney (that's not his name either) won the Amateur Championship with his Setter bitch, and after he had flushed the birds to her sixth bevy find, which everyone knew would win the stake, he was so excited that he tried three times to jump on a horse that another man was already riding!"

And so you, too, dear reader, go now and do likewise.

CHAPTER XVI

THE BREAKS OF THE GAME

THERE is no question in the writer's mind but that field trial competition represents just about the finest sport there is—particularly for those who have a deep interest in hunting dogs, whether these be Pointers, Setters, Spaniels or Beagles. Field trials can be enjoyed at seasons of the year when game may not legally be taken—thus the pleasure of sports afield is prolonged. If it were not for field trials, many of us, especially in certain sections of the country where there are short open seasons, would have our days afield cramped down to too short a number out of the three hundred and sixty-five allotted to each year.

By the very nature of the work of Spaniels, the field trials for Spaniel breeds almost require the use of the gun; but this is not necessary in trials for Bird Dogs or Hounds. Therefore, field trials for these latter breeds may be run even during legally closed seasons on game. Those of us who enjoy working our dogs in the field find that this opportunity which field trials present offers a very welcome incentive to get out in the open —an incentive that is often as keen, sometimes keener, even than hunting itself. It is all very well to enjoy working our dogs—but how much greater is that enjoyment if there is an object in view! The hunting field offers that object during the open season; and the field trial competitions supply an equally worth while objective at other seasons of the year.

There is no keener pleasure than that of making plans for a litter of puppies, raising these and watching them develop; nominating them for the Futurity, with the different championship stakes ever ahead in the offing as the ultimate goal of the All-Age performer. The keenness of anticipation is a splendid thing, often as great as the keenness of a win itself; and a field trial won against keen competition, with the trophy that will ever remain as tangible evidence of the event, will be remembered long after any mere hunt has begun to pass from the picture. The deeds of your good dog in field trials are recorded in black and white. They are written into the records—into the history of the breeds. A hunt may be a wonderful thing, as I am well aware, but a hunt is a private performance—while in field trials you show your good dog to the world!

But one must go into field trials—any competition, in fact—prepared to accept the bitter with the sweet, to take the breaks as they come and *play the game* as a sportsman should. Unless you are prepared to do this, you might as well stay out of the competitions. The breaks of the game are a determining factor in any competition—in golf—in baseball—football—and especially so in field trials. There are bound to be bitter days—days when the breaks just won't come your way. But the true sportsman will always continue to play the game, knowing that the breaks will balance and that the average is bound to be even at the end of the score.

During what was perhaps the largest major circuit field trial for Pointers and Setters during the past season, I saw a very definite evidence of the way the breaks of the game are almost sure to balance. A friend of mine had entered two of his splendid Setters in the Open All-Age Stake. Toward the end of the heat of the first of his dogs to run, the dog was out on a wide cast and my friend misjudged his whereabouts. I had seen the dog cross the road and pass into a thick woods. My friend had gone back to look for the dog in another direction and the judges delegated me to handle in his absence. I rode into those woods, but became entangled in a triangular enclosure hemmed in by barbed wire. Too much time was lost in getting out of there and by that time the dog's regular handler had arrived. I went with him to try and locate his Setter. Farther on, on the side of a hill, as I reined in my horse to take in the situation and try to estimate the dog's likely whereabouts, a single quail flushed from in front of my horse's hoofs. Shortly after that we located the dog just a short distance ahead and he was moving on. I have a very strong suspicion personally that this dog had been on point for some time—that the birds had finally flushed wild, all except the one outlying single which my horse had kicked out. But all this is only surmise. There was no find under judgment. The dog was not called back into the Second Series.

Now that was a tough break of the luck. Who knows but that we might have found that dog on point had we gotten to him sooner! Sure it was tough luck—just as it's tough luck in a golf game when a good shot strikes a tree and bounces out of bounds—and just as it's good luck if that same ball should chance to bounce in bounds and nearer the green instead. So also is there good luck in field trials just as there is bad luck. Let me recite the opposite of the incident just related.

In that same field trial, as I have already said, my same friend had another Setter entered. This dog also ran a good heat. His range was splendid. His speed was supreme. His hunting judgment was good. But toward the end of the heat this dog also was lost when we came to some heavy cover at the end of the course. My friend rode out to find him, but his estimate of the dog's direction was wrong. Just before they were about to start the next brace, my friend rode back with the announcement that he had not found his dog. He knew that they had been ordered up.

But what he did not know was that someone else had found the dog within the time limit—had found him pointing birds and doing it well—that this find had come under judgment—and that the dog's manners were satisfactory when the birds were flushed and the blank shot fired. Thus this second dog came back into the Second Series. And thus was it proved that the breaks of the game will always balance. So don't go into field trials and then soon quit just because the early breaks are bad. Stick to the game as a sportsman should and then you will surely some day see the turning of the tide—that is, if you are entering dogs that *deserve to win.* It takes an awful lot of luck for the mediocre performer to win over a class dog.

Professional and Amateur

These are terms that are not always thoroughly understood in field trials. Furthermore, the conception also varies in different parts of the country.

The most common interpretation, however, and perhaps the most logical, is to qualify the handler rather than the dog. Thus, when we refer to an Amateur Field Trial, we most generally have reference to the handlers. In a few sections, particularly in certain parts of the South, the restriction is upon the dog as well as the handler. Thus, a dog which has been placed in an open trial may be barred thereafter from competing in an amateur trail. According to this interpretation an amateur dog may compete in an open trial—but he becomes a professional dog the minute he wins a place in such a stake. Thereafter his competition must be confined to open stakes only.

This is not, however, the interpretation of professional and amateur as understood by The Amateur Field Trial Clubs of America. According to the by-laws of this governing association, it is the handler and not the dog who is either a professional or an amateur. A professional handler is defined as anyone who has trained or handled dogs for money. Such a person is a professional and is not eligible to handle a dog either in his quali-

Pretty Work on Pheasants in New York State

fying win or in the championship itself.

But any dog, regardless of his wins, is eligible to compete in the Amateur Championship Stake of America, provided his handler at the time of the win which qualified him for this stake was an amateur; and provided he is handled by an amateur in the championship. No win when he is handled by a professional can ever qualify him for the championship—and a qualifying win must be made in a licensed stake.

An amateur is still an amateur if he enters his own dogs in an open trial and he may run in such a trial for the cash prize and keep it if he wins with his own dog—and he still remains an amateur. He may even handle a dog for some friend in such an open trial, but in this case if he accepts the cash prize or any part thereof, if he wins, he then becomes a professional. If, however, he wins with a dog for a friend and turns the full and complete prize money over to the owner, he is still an amateur. The distinction is that to remain an amateur he must neither accept cash nor its equivalent as a consideration for having performed the service of either training or handling. By handling just for the fun of it he remains an amateur. By handling for a reward he becomes a professional. But he is entitled to any kind of prize, cash or otherwise, that he may win with his own dogs and this doesn't affect his amateur standing.

Inasmuch as most amateur field trials to-day are run under the auspices of The Amateur Field Trial Clubs of America, especially the most important ones, the conception of amateur and professional as defined by this association is that which is most generally accepted all over the country. Thus the National Open Champion may also, by winning the title, become the Amateur Champion of America. It is the man, and not the dog, upon whom the restriction is placed.

CHAPTER XVII

PENNSYLVANIA GROUSE DOGS

"THOSE fellows in Pennsylvania have the best dogs I have seen in America," thus spoke a man whose early experiences with gun dogs had been acquired in Europe, but who now is one of the most prosperous trainers on this side of the Atlantic.

I knew then, and still know, that this man knows dogs. And yet I passed off the remark rather lightly with the feeling that he was perhaps taking in too much territory. One can hear so many things regarding dogs! Matured fanciers protect themselves by letting most of it go in one ear and out the other. Almost every individual—and groups of individuals from different sections—invariably believe that the dogs they know best are supreme. But now and again there comes a voice of such definite authority that we are compelled to stop and listen and heed. Such is the case in point.

In my own State, I have a friend whom I

regard as one of the finest sportsmen I have ever seen. During the past active season for field trials and hunting, he and I were together on several occasions. Following the Pheasant Championship at Buffalo, we got to discussing the Grouse Dogs of Pennsylvania. A recent Pennsylvania Grouse Champion had run in the stake we had just witnessed and his showing had scarcely been impressive.

"But you ought to see him in the woods," my friend said. "He's a different dog then. The woods inspire him—for Grouse is his game. He doesn't go wide, of course, but he's fast as a streak of greased lightning! In open cover, he is just a dog somewhat above the average; but put him in timber and he's a champion in every sense of the word. It makes all the difference in the world—but seeing is believing and you've got to go to a Pennsylvania Grouse Trial to be convinced."

Several months later, this same friend and myself were together during the National Championship at Grand Junction, Tennessee. I mention this fact especially to show that his experience is not limited to any one section of the country nor to any one type of game or type of dog. He has seen them all and he is both a keen student and an excellent judge of any kind of gun dog in any and all conditions. Again at Grand Junction, we fell to discussing the Grouse Trials and the Grouse Dogs of Pennsylvania.

"When you consider," he said, "that these dogs hunt with as much speed as any dog will show in any field trial anywhere, yet handle with never a word spoken, plunging through thickets and dodging trees, swiftly searching for the body scent of the alluring game they seek, responding instantly to the slightest motion signal from their handler, yet hunting independently all the time—you will get some conception of what the highest type of Grouse Dog is like. Of course, they quarter the cover—and don't go so wide—but that is the only difference."

The description thrilled me. The Grouse Dogs are not like that in all parts of the country. Conceptions differ in connection with Grouse Dogs perhaps more than is the case with any other type of gun dog. I have in mind one very well-known grouse hunter who insists upon his dog never breaking into a gallop. He wants the dog to trot rapidly —but it must be a trot. Never must this trot become a lope. Yet he wants the dog to seek body scent only and go to his game with high head and positive decision.

There are others who don't care so much whether the dog trots or lopes, but many of these have dogs whose lope is but a plodding gesture very much on the order of a hobby horse. Such dogs are pretty apt to be indecisive, creeping creatures that are so afraid of flushing game they sneak along following foot trails, more often ending up by flushing game than pinning it to a point. This thing of pinning game, especially certain kinds of game such as the grouse or the prairie chicken or the pheasant, is most successfully accomplished by quick, decisive action—speed arrested so suddenly that the game's only inclination is to squat before the onslaught. A creeping performance always gives the game too much opportunity to run away or fly. The bird is given too much time to collect his wits and determine upon a course of action. A dog that rushes to his game and then suddenly applies the brakes doesn't give his game a chance to think and plan out a method of evading pursuit. The squat to a point is almost automatic. Such a performance will bring some flushes, of course, especially when the wind is wrong—but never so many flushes as the indecisive, creeping performance.

Another friend of mine, who is a regular grouse hunter in the East, had a wonderful Grouse Dog in his Pointer, of John Proctor descent, and this dog was not only fast in his youth—but fairly wide. He was hunted with a bell attached to his collar—and this enabled my friend to keep track of him in the heaviest cover. But when that bell suddenly ceased its tingling, you could bet on birds.

Now in connection with these Grouse Dogs of Pennsylvania, which my friend and I had been discussing—he with whom I attended both the Pheasant and the National Championships—he made the claim that these very dogs possessed such intelligence, backed by the best Bird Dog blood lines, that most any of them could soon be widened out to conform to our conceptions of quail trials. In fact, it is true that the best Grouse Dogs of Pennsylvania carry the same blood as has flowed in the veins of the great National Champions. Just to cite one example, it might be mentioned that the double Grouse Champion, Nugym, is the grandson of the National Champion, Eugene M.

"And, furthermore, I am going to prove to you just this thing," my friend said while we were at Grand Junction in January, "for this very spring I am planning to start my own Grouse Dog in the Open All-Age Stake of the Kentucky Trials at Camp Knox. George Kramer has him now, getting ready for that event, and I'll be interested to have you see him go in open country when we meet in March."

Well, I have but recently returned, at the date of this writing, from the Kentucky trials. I saw some dogs there that started in the National Championship—including the National Champion, Mary Blue. The cream of the country competed at Camp Knox near Louisville this year—the same quality that competed for the national title at Grand Junction, only more of it. A third again as many dogs started at Camp Knox as started at Grand Junction.

Yet my friend's little Setter, which he had called a "Grouse Dog," didn't have to take off his hat to any of them. He ran as fast and as wide and as well as perhaps any dog in the stake. But that didn't surprise me quite so much as what has come later. I know that my friend knows dogs—"big" dogs—and I know that he wouldn't have started that dog at Camp Knox unless he had known that he was equal to the company he would be keeping.

Our plans to meet, however, had gone astray. My friend didn't see his dog run, because he was unavoidably detained at the last minute by business. So, knowing he would be eager for a word of the event, I wrote him the next day describing the excellent heat his dog had produced. "But," I said, "you haven't a 'Grouse Dog' any more—you may have had one once, but you have a field trial quail dog now." I doubted if my friend himself would have been quite prepared for the type of truly "big" performance which I had seen produced by this dog which had been reared and raised in the grouse country.

Now one of the most interesting things of the whole proposition has been the comment of my friend in reply to my letter. This is what he wrote:

"Thanks for your appreciation of my dog. Am sorry if I have misled you in what I call a Grouse Dog. This dog is, and has been, a perfectly trained dog on grouse. He goes just as hard and just as snappy in the woods as you saw him go there, but of course he quarters not more than one fifty or two hundred yards to the right and left of the course, cutting across from right to left about one or two hundred feet ahead of the handler. Think I told you that grouse courses follow stream beds or pipe lines and the dogs work up and down the hills on either side of the course.

"Many times when I have talked to some of my field trial friends about some of the Grouse Dogs I like I have noticed perhaps a little indifference. They do not believe or know that some of the greatest dogs living are Grouse Dogs. I did not myself till I had watched them work. There are several better dogs than mine running in the grouse trials now and I feel sure that he could not have been placed in the open grouse trials this year. If he is a good little dog, then the other fellows have better ones in my judgment and I feel sure that the grouse trials would prove it. I know one that has never been out of the woods in his life and never seen a quail and he is both wider and faster than my dog. *They have to be fast to handle grouse right.*"

I read the above—but still I wasn't convinced. I still didn't believe that my friend was right. I still felt sure that a transition had taken place—that his dog would never prove to be a 'Grouse Dog' again—at least certainly not without a great deal of slowing up and cutting down of his range over a long period of time. For part of his quail heat was run through a section bordering timber and he bored into that cover without any "quartering" such as his early grouse training would have seemed to call forth, unless the transition had been complete as I so believed. Thus I again wrote to my friend, expressing these thoughts—but again his reply was the same. Here it is:

"Hope I did not stir your sporting blood too much when I wrote you that 'Ted' is a Grouse Dog still. Now, of course, I don't think I could start him away on a grouse course and make him stay within the prescribed limits the first ten or fifteen minutes, but I know before the half hour was up he would be cutting that course like a perfect Grouse Dog should. Mind you he was only a grouse derby—not an all-age—and was placed three times out of four starts. But what I want you to know is that 'Ted' is not good enough to run in the all-age grouse stakes this year for the simple reason that I know at least six dogs in Pennsylvania that can beat him every day in the week. 'Ted' does not belong to me because I thought he was a great dog, but because he was the only one of the good dogs, Grouse Dogs all, that could be bought. It was simply a case of beggar's choice with me.

"I don't want you to think that all Grouse Dogs will go as wide as 'Ted' does now in the open, because they will not, but any of the good ones I know will go just as wide and some faster in one month of horseback work. To cite one case, I know of one dog that has never seen a quail nor a man on a horse and I put him down in big open country one day and he was as wide and much faster than Mary Blue was at Grand Junction after they had both run an hour. They will all go wide enough and nothing but a fast dog is ever a good Grouse Dog. Those fellows over there in Pennsylvania have the best Setters in the country and you can't buy them for love nor money just because they love their dogs too much to sell them.

"I hesitate to say all these things about the Grouse Dogs for I know there are a great many of my field trial friends who can't believe them and I don't much blame them. I know you are always open-minded and so hope to have the pleasure of showing you some day, simply because you will be the most pleased man in the world to find out that the general opinion of the Grouse Dog is all wrong. This in my opinion is the reason why Grouse Dogs are not looked on with favor by the quail dog men. They know that in the woods the dog must quarter at not more than two hundred yards to enable the handler to see them at all times and they naturally assume that a dog that turns that often can't be fast or much of a dog. Well, just take a tip from me, the Grouse Setters are much better dogs than either the Pointers or the Setters are quail dogs. If I ever get my hands on any of the five or six I like, I will show you all. That is not boasting, either. It is prophesy."

Ordinarily, I would consider much of the above but idle chatter. But in the present instance, such is not the case. I know the man who wrote those words—and I know full well that he knows. There is no one I know in whose opinion I would be more willing to place dependence.

CHAPTER XVIII

THE STORY OF BREAKING BETTY

THE things that come hardest in this world often prove the most worth while in the end. It seems that we must *earn* those things which are best and most desirable. It is also true that it is often darkest when nearest dawn. The story of breaking "Betty" is a case in point.

As Gun Dog Editor of *Field & Stream,* I have been keeping track of the nature of the many letters that come to me from readers asking questions pertaining to their dogs, and I find that four out of five are inquiries relative to *stanchness on point.* One will want to know what to do to make his six months old Pointer puppy hold his birds; another will want information on the same matter in connection with a Setter only eight months of age; while still others may ask for similar advice in reference to young dogs around a year old—many of them never having been in the field more than eight or ten times!

Now it is manifestly impossible in my replies to such letters to go into very deep detail. My answers must be short; yet in some cases I realize that a lengthy discussion would undoubtedly be more helpful. That is why I have chosen to write this special chapter—because I think it may prove the best answer I could give to four out of every five letters that come to me; and thus once, at least, I shall tell the entire story. The case is an extreme one, I confess, yet it should serve to show that most of us are expecting too much of our dogs too quickly. And that statement alone is the answer to most of the letters I receive.

The only way to give you the whole picture will be to start at the beginning. Betty Buckeye, as she is registered in the Field Dog Stud Book, is by Jersey Prince out of Eumogenia. Those who recognize what is best in English Setter blood lines will detect that Betty's veins carry the *blue*. Jersey Prince was a Prairie Chicken Champion. His sire was Boaz; and Boaz was by Jesse Rodfield's Count Gladstone. But it was Betty's fire and style and speed in the field that caused me to buy her when she was but ten months of age. Could I have foreseen then that it would take me almost five years before she would handle game, the question might occur to some whether I should have considered it worth while. And the answer would be *YES*—if I might also have been privileged to foresee that she would be just what she is today.

I would rather wait five years for one Betty Buckeye—than have a dozen dogs of inferior variety. For the Betty Buckeye kind are *worth waiting for*. I will admit that I should have been mighty glad had she taken to handling game at an earlier age than she has—*IF* that might have been accomplished without taking anything out of her. Ah! that's the big point. And I realize that then I might have had a longer period of pleasure with her than I can now expect. But I also realize that those things most worth while come hardest—and I stand ready to pay the price of waiting for such a dog as she.

Gee, what a kick I got out of watching Betty run and hunt and find and flush and chase! I taught her to respond to the whistle signals that we use in field trials; but she was a little demon to handle. All she ever thought about in the field was finding game—and it was hard to make her hear because of her concentration on the one thing that so absorbed her soul. She was oblivious to all else. In other words, she had the *natural qualifications* that judges are looking for in puppy stakes; and so when she turned a year of age I started her in her first field trial. But she did not win that time because we found that she had the fault of trailing. Later on I'll mention how I got her over this fault.

I noticed, however, that, although she was the worst trailer I have ever seen, she did not always do it. Thus a little later I again entered her in competition; and this time she simply smothered the stake. In my enthusiasm over her heat that day I sent her to the Prairies to be gotten ready to run as a Derby in the Manitoba and All-America prairie chicken trials the following September. All went well for a while, and I had good reports of her, and then the tune of these reports started to change. Betty wasn't running so well as she had. One day a telegram reached me which explained what was the matter. That wire read as follows: "Betty whelped one mut puppy today. Am shipping her home."

Thus had died any hope of getting her ready for the two big stakes for which her nominating fees had already been paid. Her daddy was a Chicken Champion; but Betty has never again been to the prairies since that one first trip as an early Derby—a trip so suddenly and sadly cut short. Too many of us, I think, seem to feel that matters pertaining to our dogs must be all fair sailing; but it is seldom so and we must not let discouragement dishearten us. That is one of the first lessons that every Bird Dog man must learn. Too many of us are faint hearted enthusiasts.

When Betty reached home, as soon as she was in shape for the field again, I began to work her myself in preparation for the Derby stake of the Miami Valley field trials. In that stake she went into the second series with a slight edge over her litter brother, and the judges kept them down for over an hour in direct competition, running for first and second. Finally her brother found a bevy of birds; thus he was awarded first and Betty second.

Up to this time but very little effort had been made to get Betty to point. The important thing was to develop her speed and range and *experience in finding game.* It made but little difference whether she flushed her birds or not—learning where to search was the foremost fundamental. Any pressure of restraint had been very gentle. But she was now almost two years old and I began gradually to bear down on her. She had made quite a number of flash points; but never stayed with them long. Never long enough for me to get to her—and that is what I now so needed to do. If I could just get my hands on her once, I knew that a mighty step toward the desired end would be taken. I could then *make clear to her* what was wanted. And that is all-essential. Yet getting to Betty proved something easier discussed than accomplished. It always is so in the case of a wide, fast, eager dog. You've got to wait for the right opportunity. And you might add a bit of prayer to the waiting.

But the chance I sought never came my way

—the breaks never favored me. One day I had Betty out for a walk. I was all dressed up like a new church, for some unaccountable reason, so I kept to the railroad track and let Betty get her exercise by running the adjoining fields. Suddenly I saw her point. I spoke to her and she held. A deep embankment separated us. It was full of briars. I thought of my new clothes—and thus lost a golden opportunity to have accomplished something. Then my sluggish mind began to function. My suit was not worth more than sixty dollars; yet I'd gladly have given twice that to accomplish the breaking of Betty Buckeye. When reason thus dawned, Betty was still holding her birds. I gave her a final word of caution—and jumped into the ditch beyond the track. But my mind had functioned too late—for when I emerged the birds had gone, and Betty with them.

Thus it went on time after time. Once I was working her from horseback. I saw her flash into a point far in the distance. I put spurs to my steed and dashed toward her. But she couldn't wait for me. I was too far from her, so she put up her birds and ran them out of the country. From the rate she was going when last seen, I imagine she must have been right with them when they settled. But this is only surmise.

I planned to hunt three weeks in Alabama that February. It was a long, hard winter and the deep snow at home made it impossible to work dogs, so I sent Betty to a trainer in Tennessee. He had been able to accomplish little or nothing with her when she was shipped to me in Alabama. Just about the time I began to work her in Alabama she came in season. The Setter with which I decided to mate her is a field trial Champion. I left Betty with his handler, instructing him to breed her and then to keep and work her for six or seven weeks before the puppies should arrive. She came home in due time showing very little signs of having been worked; the only report accompanying her being that she was an incurable trailer.

Perhaps I might now mention how I cured her of trailing. No dog is ever incurable of anything if properly handled. Some of them may not be worth the effort, that I admit. But I maintain that not enough effort of the right sort is expended in the case of some of them. I worked Betty *alone* a great deal. This is one way to cure a trailer. Left to their own initiative, they learn to develop independence. I also tried something else. I worked her a great deal with an older, much slower dog, one lacking also her natural range. This had a good effect. Betty was so much faster and wider that she just couldn't be bothered by hanging back for him. Thus she began to run her own heats with no more signs of trailing. Time alone—if we will but spend enough of it—is a great curer; and in time I found that I could run Betty with dogs as fast and wide as herself and still she did not trail. If she ever did, it was rarely—and never for long.

Well, I had cured her of trailing—a worse fault than not pointing, at her age—so I began to get lots of kick out of the great heats she ran. She was now an All-Age dog and would have to point and handle birds to win in any field trial. But she was running so well I entered her in one stake anyhow, just for the fun of it, and hoped she wouldn't find birds. She didn't. But she ran such a big heat that the judges called her back into the second series on class. I was glad she found no birds; but I got a keen thrill out of handling her on that occasion.

But a Bird Dog that won't point birds is about as useless as a sore tooth; and Betty was getting to the place where she would have tried the patience of Job. I gave up the idea of fast short heats and began working her down in longer heats. The whole plan now was to get her to point and handle game. Unless she could be brought to perform her main mission in life, she would be useless as a field dog, speed or no speed, range or no range, style or no style. So the art of handling game now became my sole object with her. Still, I am in the unfortunate position of having to make a living and thus could devote only week ends to the job at hand with Betty.

I placed her with a local trainer to be worked every day and I joined him every week end. He tried everything. He worked her on a long lead for control. He worked her sometimes alone; at other times with broken dogs. Yet he made no headway that

Stanch as They Make 'Em—the English Setter Bitch, Betty Buckeye, Pointing Quail in Mississippi, January 30th, 1932

anyone could notice. Taken up on lead behind a pointing dog, she simply sulked at the restraint. She made no pretense of honoring such finds. Restraint killed her interest. The proposition began to assume discouraging proportions. Two factors, however, spurred me to go on. One was a fascination and love for Betty; and the other was that the very difficulty seemed to prod me as a challenge to conquer and win out against the odds.

There was an English trainer in a nearby state and it occurred to me that perhaps his experience in discipline might be just the thing needed in this case. So I made arrangements for him to take Betty. He had her from March to November. During the summer he gave her a course of yard breaking. We both thought this might be a good idea. Yet I never got a very encouraging report. He did finally claim he could make Betty hold birds if close enough to her—but that she would always pop them when far out. He offered one excuse for her and that was that he thought she had a weak nose—he didn't believe she could smell them properly. That was a new angle, for my idea had always been that Betty had a good nose, and I never did accept the belief to the contrary. Yet I confess there were times when I wavered.

Betty came back to me the first of November. Our shooting season opened in fifteen days and I worked her hard hoping for results. I got none. One day she made a find not too far from me. It was in plain view so that I saw it all. Had there been even the slightest chance for doubt, I should have given her the benefit of that doubt and withheld punishment. But there was no doubt. Her flushing and chasing had been as deliberate as could be. So I brought her back to the exact spot and punished her hard. She sulked and seemed actually to defy me. Matters were rapidly getting no better. I had just one repetition after another of the same sort of situation. I, too, now began to wonder if a weak nose might be at the bottom of it. Perhaps she did not detect location with sufficient distinctness. Yet all this while the challenge kept taunting me to go on; and I made this assertion time after time: "I'm going to break her if it takes me until she's nine years old."

Which brings us to the month of January—with Betty then lacking but two months of being five years old. Yet I carried her to Mississippi with me, still hoping for better luck down there. "Hope," you know, "springs eternal in the human breast." What I begged and prayed for was a situation that would permit me a chance to give the little bitch a word of praise. Restraint was beginning to get her goat. She was as frayed at the edges as I was myself. Nothing but scolding; nothing but punishment in the field; no chance to let her know that hunting for a master can really be a happy proposition. All she had ever seen of it had given her trouble. You couldn't kill the hunting instinct in her—the blood of Jersey Prince was too potent for that. But it was mighty easy for me to detect that I was killing the joy of being *with me* in the field. Yet the strange thing is that she never bolted—not once—and I have often marveled thereat. I know that Betty loved me and she was the dearest little thing you ever saw when we were not afield. All she asked then was to be let alone to hunt as *she* pleased; and all I asked was that she do something that would please *me.* If we could only get on a footing of mutual understanding, I knew I'd win out. She would have wanted to please me—but she just didn't know how; and I had never been able to make clear to her how much she had to gain thereby. The great art in training lies in making things clear to a dog. A dog in confusion as to what is expected of him cannot perform properly—and can scarcely be blamed. But Betty's purposes and mine kept far apart. We just couldn't seem to get together. And her disposition afield was getting worse faster than I cared to admit.

Then came a day when she actually blinked a bevy. I was close to her at the time and she feared to take her medicine. Instead of the usual flush and chase, she just passed them up entirely and sneaked away. I caught her at it when the Irish Setter bitch which is the queen of my heart came that way shortly and pointed the birds right where Betty had blinked them. This blinking business was not only bad—it was *the worst yet;* for blinking is often the most fatal of all faults.

The next day I again caught Betty blinking. Furthermore, she was sulkier than I had ever seen her. She seemed just to defy me openly and wantonly. She as much as said: "Go on—do your damndest and see if I care!" The sweetest dog you ever saw around the kennel; the most sullen under restraint in the field! I think one of the reasons I had kept working with her was my keen admiration for her pure guts. Gentle, as a rule—but bold and game in the field. She paid no attention to cuts or injury. No bleeding foot ever stopped Betty Buckeye. And no sportsman can fail to thrill to courage—now can you? I never have heard Betty even whimper under punishment. She simply seemed to say: "Well, go on and let's get this over with!" And so I admired even as I damned her.

But there is an end even to the patience of Job. Enough is enough of anything. And so, soon after the blinking started, I gave up the ghost with Betty Buckeye. Came a day when I said to Lucius Waldrip: "Well, I'm through. For good and all—and unconditionally—I'm forever through. I quit right here. I have said I'd break her if it took me nine years—but I've changed my mind.

Life's too short. I'll find a good home for her; but my kennel has no room for any but *bird dogs."* So we took Betty back to the house and put her up. And right then, with my mind free, I began to enjoy the hunt over my other dogs with a joy such as I could not know while brooding over Betty.

Now Lucius and I had planned to run up to Grand Junction for the National Championship. So he said to me one evening: "I'll have to get my nephew to come over and stay while we're away. Tomorrow morning we'll ride over to my brother's and arrange it."

And as we were about to start that next morning, I said: "Well, Betty hasn't been out for several days and needs exercise. Since we'll not be hunting, I'll let her follow us for a run—I must be fair to her anyway." Yet I stuck my gun in the scabbard always hanging from my saddle.

We rode over and made the necessary arrangements to "keep the home fires burning" while we were away, and Betty ranged all over the map on both sides of the road from us. On the way home Lucius suggested that we turn in at a likely looking field and see if we might run into a bevy. Even though Betty flushed them, he felt that we might be able to mark down and kill three or four birds for supper.

Betty took one of her customary wide casts to the left and swung out far ahead of us. Suddenly she started to cut back, but stopped and stood seemingly watching us. I paid little or no attention to her, but rode straight on. As I passed her, I noticed that she did not glance up at me—but seemed to be looking past me. But I didn't bother to pay much attention. I didn't know what she was doing and didn't care. I had *given her up.* I did, however, turn and look back after we had ridden on a short distance and I saw Betty pull down the field a couple hundred yards—then turn and swing back up against the wind. Suddenly she stopped stone still with head and tail on high. She was as solid as you've ever seen 'em.

Lucius exclaimed: "Well now for the life of me—would you look at that. She's *got 'em!*"

"Yes, but she won't have them long," I answered and made no move to turn back. I'd *given her up,* you see.

But Lucius wouldn't have it that way—perhaps because he hadn't suffered with her as much as I had. "Well, if you won't, I will," he said—and turned his horse around. Betty was still holding.

So I turned my horse also, and rode toward her. I did one thing different than I ever had before. Because I no longer cared, I failed to caution her as on all previous occasions. Whether or not this had anything to do with it, I do not know—but I am now inclined to think that in her particular case it may have. I did not repeat my customary command to "Whoa." Instead, I got off and tied my horse, taking my time, took my gun from the scabbard and approached the point —little expecting to get close enough for a shot. But Betty stuck to her guns—and, gentlemen, she *had 'em.* In a flash my whole attitude changed. Back surged my old desire, that had been dormant for the past few days. I shot to kill—and thank goodness, I did—and Betty saw me do it. She saw me do something she herself had never been able to do—stop a bird. Yet she had played a part in it, too—a big part. She had seen that it pays to play team work. It was the first such experience of her life. It *is* a long lane that has no turning; and the breaks had at last come my way!

Of course Betty broke shot—and she kept on going. I stood still and tried to whistle her in. But she was afraid to come to me. All her life she had done wrong; hence all her life to be whistled in meant for punishment, varying anywhere from mild to severe. So punishment is what she was expecting now. A great deal depended on how I handled the situation.

Lucius said: "You'll have to go get her and bring her back."

"No," I replied, "I shall not. I'll stay right here until she comes in to me, if it takes all afternoon. And then when she does come in, I shall show her something she has never known before—the reward and joy that come with doing right. This is my great chance to distinguish for her the difference between right and wrong—so that she may know that difference always hereafter."

And, as I stood there, Betty came in to me—on her stomach, I admit, and squirming along only a few inches at a time. But I stood right where the birds had been and she reached me at last. Then I knelt down and took her in my arms. I hugged—and even kissed—her. I talked to her and crooned over her. Certainly this was better than punishment!—and it could not have helped but register with Betty.

But had it? That remained to be seen. All pepped up again now—and with the lightest heart I had ever known while working Betty—we remounted and rode on. There's no use to hold you in suspense. Yes, Betty found and handled perfectly two more bevies before we reached the house; and, as I was shooting for high stakes, I killed on each occasion, thus driving the lesson home; and each time, too, she was shown, as in the first place, the payment of petting that all dogs love so much and which is the reward for doing well.

That night even the stars seemed to shine with a deeper meaning. But I just *had* to postpone our trip to Grand Junction while I tested Betty again to see if the thing that had happened the day before was destined to endure. It did. Betty made one find of her own and backed five other finds by the older dogs that I worked with her. More than that —she did the prettiest, stanchest backing I have almost ever seen. She honored each point promptly at sight and never budged an inch. There was no crowding in nor attempt to steal—no manifest jealousy such as often spoils otherwise perfect performances in the field. When I had seen all this, I was ready to go to the National Championship.

All the time we were away I kept thinking of Betty and could scarcely wait to get back to her again and go on with the good work. I planned to hunt the last four days of the season in Mississippi before starting home. And not one of those four days did Betty disappoint me. I shall never hunt her again quite that hard. No fast dog should be hunted four days running, even though they were but half day heats. Still, for just this once I think it was justified—and it was the end of the season. The last day I hunted her with Smada Byrd and killed my limit over those two bitches by noon—and the last two bevies were found by Betty Buckeye, with Smada Byrd doing the backing, and that's going some. So by one o'clock we were packing up to start our long trek homeward.

Before I felt justified, however, in publishing the story of these experiences one thing more remained to be done. It was essential to test Betty out in Northern cover and see if she could be counted on to keep the good work going. This account was not even begun until after this test had been made. The first Saturday after getting home Betty ran one of the finest heats I have ever seen her produce—and she *finished on birds.* Furthermore, these were pinned in an open corn field. The birds began to run as I approached—and I am sure that Betty, too, could see them running. That is the most trying sort of situation even for the stanchest dogs. Yet Betty never budged. That same night I started to type this story—for I knew that Betty was broken. If anything goes wrong now, it will be *my* fault—not hers. The handler who can't keep a dog that far along on the straight and narrow path—has no business to be handling dogs. And I flatter myself too much to lack any faith in the future.

Now what can we learn from all this? We should learn something if the story is worth telling. We can learn this—that we should not begin to worry because our six months old, or ten months old, or twelve months old, or eighteen months old, or even twenty-four months old puppies aren't yet handling game. That's one thing we *should* learn. Another thing is this: We must learn to handle dogs before we expect them to fill our heart's desire. As one old trainer once put it: "No one can train a dog unless he knows more than the dog."

One error was made with Betty that is always bad. Too many trainers had worked on her before I got down to business with her myself. Don't be changing trainers—except for real cause. I do not blame the trainers to whom I sent Betty. None of them had her long enough. There were reasons for this in the present case—but the rule holds good. Take plenty of time in advance to pick your trainer—then when you pick him *stick to him*. Always starting over again never leads anywhere.

By cramping Betty, she might have been broken earlier. But that would have kept her out of field trials as a puppy and derby—and who wants them cramped anyhow! However, I am beginning to lean toward not running keen Setters in field trials as puppies and derbies. If the breaking is done first—provided it is done in a way not to take too much out of them—they can be widened out again later. With Pointers it doesn't make so much difference. They break younger—and easier.

Another lesson we may learn from this story is that the dogs most worth waiting for usually *must* be waited for. All this business of cheap dogs and quick training—the impatience for results before results are due—simply ends up in misconceptions and dogs that *are* cheap—in value as well as price. We must learn, too, not to expect some trainer to finish in six months a dog that is destined to require two years if he is to be finished *right.* We're usually in too much of a hurry! *We must learn to wait.*

Training takes time. I admit that in Betty's case it took too much time. I confess, as I have already admitted, that I had even given up all hope for her. But she was almost five years old—and her high strung disposition had, under restraint, developed some of the worst faults a dog may acquire. Blinking being perhaps the one *worst* fault. Of course I was lucky in that Betty came to herself just in time to escape the discard. Then —and this was important—I grasped the opportunity that was presented and made the most of it. This had a great deal to do with the fact that after that one first point there was no back sliding.

The important fact is that I now have a real one. Betty Buckeye is almost five years old as this is written—and will be turned five before it can appear in print. But she has proved worth waiting for. Since this manuscript was started she has continued her stanchness and has been handling game regularly.

If you don't fancy the keen ones—and some don't—then sell such and buy one of the more easy going type. This is much better than to try to force the keen kind to come too quickly. But do not be misled. Don't mistake a never-will-be and wait in the hope of later joy which may never come. You want to be sure and know what's really *inside* the dog and whether he's worth the waiting. You don't want to wait and then end up by experiencing such disappointment as I came so mighty close to knowing. I hope you never may.

CHAPTER XIX

DOG WHISTLE SIGNALS

AN OLD hunter came in to see me one day and suggested that a campaign to promote a uniformity in the use of dog whistles would be mighty helpful. His idea was to encourage trainers all to use the same signals and also promote a wider understanding of these among dog owners. As a matter of fact the trainers already do follow pretty much the same code —differing only about as one human voice varies from another in quality and tone. What every owner should charge himself to acquire is the closest possible imitation of the signals to which the dog was trained, as well as an understanding of the very simple basic code.

The first time I ever took a long trip away from home for a quail hunt (with a borrowed pointer, which in itself was a mistake, for no man should ever borrow a dog—but that was many years ago and before I knew any better), I secured for myself a tiny tin whistle, which I carried tied to my hunting coat. Frankly, it wasn't a dog whistle. It just made a tooting sort of sound that didn't reach far enough for any wide dog to hear. In fact, the dog I had was a really good one and he could never hear that whistle except when he was right fairly close to me—and when a dog is that close there's little or no occasion to use a whistle at all. You might better speak to him.

Furthermore, I had no more idea than the dead how any sort of dog whistle should be used. That dog wasn't acquainted either with the whistle—or the way I used it—or with me. In fact, I knew nothing about whistle signals, was not aware that a whistle might be used for any other purpose than to call a dog in. And a dog not accustomed to that strange little whistle I was using could not possibly have known what it meant. In fact, it had no meaning at all. But there I was just the same—a hunter with an inadequate new whistle and a borrowed dog. I still recall that my two companions and myself were dumb enough not to realize why the dog seemed neither to understand nor to heed my varied and impotent tooting efforts.

I once saw a novice handler at a field trial

decked out with enough whistles for two or three men. He had wooden whistles and metal whistles. The wooden whistles were painted different colors. He had prepared himself to do some real whistling, and did—till a judge called him down.

In giving a dog a command of any kind, it is important that the dog should previously be trained to know the meaning of the command as given. This is just as important in the case of whistling at him as it is in the case of giving him an order by voice. He must be acquainted with the tone of the whistle itself—as well as with the meaning of the several whistle signals. It is also important to use the same whistle and not keep changing on him. No field trial handler would ever think of borrowing a whistle. He knows that there is just enough difference in the notes of different whistles so that the dog might be confused.

We've all seen men who whistle through their fingers in handling a dog. The trouble with that is you can't get sufficient change of pace or variety of tone. And the little tin whistles that merely toot are not adapted for handling a dog, except possibly a close one in the woods for grouse. A wide dog on quail in the South or chickens on the prairies would soon be beyond the range of these tiny tooters.

The most generally accepted and serviceable whistle is the Acme Thunderer. They come either nickel-plated or bakelite. I very much prefer the latter. If you suddenly use a metal whistle on a very cold day, your lips may stick to it and take off the skin.

The fundamental whistle signals are quite simple. Unfortunately it isn't so easy to describe them as it would be by actual demonstration with a real whistle. Quickly stated, however, the three fundamental signals are as follows: Two short-sharp notes given closely together means to go on. The very way it is given tends to urge a dog. The two notes are sounded close together and so sharply that the tendency is to push the dog forward. If the signal is well taught, it is possible in time to send a dog on out farther from any distance. A longer, drawn-out single note is to attract the dog's attention so as to give him a signal by motion of the hand to turn him in some different direction. When you have attracted his attention by the whistle, you motion him the way you want him to go and then give him the go-out signal to start him in the direction as indicated. The third and last signal is a long-drawn-out, prolonged whistling, which is to call the dog in. The voice of the whistle almost seems to say, "Come in." It is more natural for the dog to respond to the come-in signal than the go-out signal. Hence the former is the easier to teach. The dog will learn the meaning of this with almost no effort on your part. If trainers will use these signals in training, and if owners will use them thereafter, it would indeed, as suggested be a good thing from every angle—and particularly so for the dog. Most trainers do use them. It simply remains for owners to learn to use them in the same way when handling their dogs.

But after all, the trouble with too set a formula—with whistles or any other angles of dog training and handling—is that most all of us have peculiarities of our own; and individual dog temperaments often may call for some variation of practice. For instance, I know that on my own part I have fallen into a habit of not using the two short-sharp notes if the dog is going nicely—the short-sharp notes being more definite, so to speak, and I hold that signal in reserve to push a dog if he should start to slump. For the dog going nicely, but which I simply wish to give a touch of encouragement to keep on, I find myself using just a soothing single note with a little tone to it slightly difficult to describe. But I find my dogs quickly get on to it and never confuse it with either a stopping or come-in signal. It is because of this possibility for individuality that any special campaign for too firmly set signals might fall short.

In the above connection I recall hearing Bob Bevan discussing at the English Setter Club field trials at Medford, New Jersey, his use of the whistle in handling the famous pointer, Seaview Rex. Bevan smiled and said: "I don't think any competing handler could turn him." By that he meant that if Rex was in competition and should hear a competing handler whistle to his own dog, he would not confuse it with his own handler's whistle but would keep on uninterruptedly with his work. There again you have that matter of individuality. Though two handlers might be using a whistle—and though both might be using the same make of whistle —Bevan had no fear whatsoever that Seaview Rex would be confused by signals by a competing handler. The way two men use a whistle will be as distinctively individual as one man's golf stroke from another's.

When all is said and done, however, although a complete uniformity in the matter of whistle signals may not be either possible or desirable, nevertheless, I do feel convinced that the fundamentals need no change and that the more uniform their use may become, the better it will be for trainers, handlers and dogs. There may be exceptions to all rules—but perhaps that is only a good way to prove the rule. Certain it is that any owner will make a mistake who gets his dog from a trainer and then fails to use the same whistle signals that the dog has been taught to understand—and as closely as it is possible to imitate.

Make it a point, therefore, to question your trainer carefully on this score and learn from him what signals he has been using, and copy them. In fact, I might add that you should learn from him anything else that you can of any special methods he has used in handling your dog. It is failure to do this that often leads to owners having poor success with their dogs when they come back from trainers. If you can't spend a day or two with the trainer and the dog in the field before attempting to handle yourself, you should at least come as close as you can to getting full and complete information by mail.

There is one thing certain and that is that if you know the fundamental use of a dog whistle, you won't go far wrong, and it is based on this very fact that one handler can often take a strange dog and get along at least fairly well with him—provided the handler himself is experienced and can quickly get the "feel" of the dog. If that statement should sound a bit mysterious—old dog men or trainers will know what I mean.

Some few handlers use two whistles, and in this case one is exclusively for the go-out signal and the other to bring the dog in. This idea is all right, but there are many hunters who may not want to go to the bother of carrying two whistles, and it isn't really necessary if you use the one whistle to convey the different meanings as outlined. There will be different uses, of course, if you are handling a retriever, beagle or spaniel. The signals as given are those commonly in use in handling pointers and setters. There is scarcely any breed of hunting dog with which the use of a whistle in some form or another doesn't enter the game. It is surprising what intelligence a good dog will develop in responding to the whistle signals.

Make a practice whenever you cut a dog loose for a hunt to accompany the release with the two-note whistle signal—two short, sharp toots in quick succession. You do this as the dog is naturally going away from you to start hunting. By keeping it up long enough, the dog will learn to associate these signals with going away—so that the time will come when the dog will understand them and respond even when they are given and he is out ahead working and you want to send him on farther.

Now suppose you have had a dog hunting and you're through. You start a prolonged whistling. If he doesn't understand at first, at least his attention is attracted and his curiosity aroused and he should swing around toward you to see what it is all about. You then call him if he is in range of your voice. You alternate such calls with a continuance of the whistling. Between the two, he understands that you want him to come in. If you are standing still, his almost natural tendency is to come in. Because you do not move on, he grasps the idea of coming to you. By continuance of this practice he will come to understand the prolonged whistle as the come-in signal, and in due time can be induced to respond to it alone—provided he hasn't any bolting tendencies.

Assured perfection comes after plenty of practice. As in all dog training matters, however, you must use good judgment. Never *overdo* anything. Don't whistle just to hear yourself do it. Don't ask a dog to keep coming to your signal just to be doing it. I never ask a dog to do anything that doesn't make sense. If it does make sense, he *must* do it. Otherwise you but belittle yourself in his eyes. When I speak of practice, I mean from day to day—not all in a heap at one time. That's simply silly, and any dog knows that it is. He'll lose respect for you—and never obey so well. Say you're working a pup or young dog, and good reason presents to give him the come-in whistle—maybe he's out of sight, or far out, and time's come to quit—now you whistle him in, and reward him with praise for compliance. That's all there is to it. One such lesson a day may suffice. There's always another day. Never be constantly nagging a dog. Too many men do. Be firm—but fair.

There isn't much to teaching the attention signal. The very sharp whistle naturally attracts attention—and that just about tells the whole story. Only a very hard-headed dog will fail to heed and respond—but that's something else again.

There are two other signals used commonly in field trials that I have found most useful, too, when hunting. Suppose a dog is lost for a time and you go one way to look for him, while your companion goes in another direction. One of you finds him—the signal to the other that you have is three loud notes on the whistle. This is mighty helpful when beyond the range of voice from one another. It gives both your location and that of the dog so that your partner may join you. Those with whom I hunt, and myself, are constantly using this signal to much advantage.

The next signal is four notes similar to the above—but *four,* not merely three. This means, not only that you have found the dog—but that he is *on point.* If your partner can come up in time, he may get in on the shooting. This one's a honey—as you'll find, too, if you use it.

But mainly—above all else and always—the big thing is that the dog, your companion—and yourself—should know and not vary the signals understood between you. Whatever the special signals you use may not matter—but complete mutual understanding of them is everything.